THE COMMON LAW LIBRARY

NUMBER 10

PHIPSON ON EVIDENCE

THIRD CUMULATIVE SUPPLEMENT TO THE THIRTEENTH EDITION

BY

M. N. HOWARD, M.A., B.C.L.

one of Her Majesty's Counsel

PETER CRANE, M.A., LL.B., LL.M.

of Gray's Inn; a Circuit Judge on the Midland and Oxford Circuit

Up to date to August 1, 1986

LONDON

SWEET & MAXWELL

Published in 1987 by
Sweet and Maxwell Limited of
11 New Fetter Lane, London
and printed in Great Britain
by The Eastern Press Limited
of London and Reading

Main Work ISBN 0 421 26990 1
Supplement ISBN 0 421 37070 X

TABLE OF CASES

TABLE OF STATUTES

[Paragraph references in **bold** indicate where a section is set out.]

PHIPSON ON EVIDENCE

THIRD SUPPLEMENT TO THE THIRTEENTH EDITION

EDITORS' NOTE: As Senior Editor of the last three editions of *Phipson on Evidence*, Judge John Buzzard took a very active part in the revision of the main work and the preparation of Supplements. His death in January 1984, has deprived us of the benefit of his energy and scholarship, and is a great loss not only to us personally but to all who use and work with *Phipson*.

CHAPTER 1.—INTRODUCTORY

View, search, physical examination, fingerprints, etc.

1–15 Add NOTE 58a. The view must also take place in the presence of the judge: *R.* v. *Hunter* [1985] 2 All E.R. 173 (C.A.). That was a case where witnesses were present at the view, but it is submitted that the decision applies to all views, and that dicta in *Tameshwa* v. *R.* which suggest that a more relaxed rule obtained in relation to views where no witnesses are present are wrong (the Court of Appeal in the instant case doubted their correctness).

NOTE 61. Add *Parry* v. *Boyle* [1986] Crim.L.R. 551 (D.C.). Lay justices should comply with the principle in *Salsbury* v. *Woodland* (see text): they should not carry out a view or inspection without the parties being present. (Compare their ability to rely on their own local knowledge: see text §§ 2–08 to 2–09.)

NOTE 65. All common law and statutory powers (with the exception of those arising under the Prevention of Terrorism (Temporary Provisions) Act 1984) to search persons at police stations have been abolished and replaced by those contained in the Police and Criminal Evidence Act, sections 53–55 and Annex A to the Code of Practice for the Detention, Treatment and Questioning of Persons by the Police.

NOTE 74. For intimate searches see the Police and Criminal Evidence Act, sections 55 and Annex A to the Code of Practice for the Detention, Treatment and Questioning of Persons by the Police. For compulsory fingerprinting, see sections 61, 65, Code of Practice for the Identification of Persons, para. 3.

1–19 NOTE 88. Add to footnote: and *cf. Savings and Investment Bank* v. *Gasco B.V.* [1984] 1 W.L.R. 271 where Peter Gibson J. (at p. 278) said that even judges should not have to perform the mental gymnastics of ruling evidence inadmissible and then trying to ignore it. The scepticism expressed in the footnote to the text as to the correctness in *R.* v. *Reynolds* appears to have received some support from the decision in *R.* v. *Goldstein* [1982] 1 W.L.R. 804 (C.A.), where it was held that the principle that a hearing must take place in open court is not necessarily to be applied where a question of pure law for the judge falls to be decided.

In magistrates' courts, where the tribunal unites the functions of trier of fact and adjudicator on legal questions, it is not appropriate to hold a trial within a trial in order to determine whether or not evidence is admissible. Thus, magistrates who refused to hear further argument about an issue they had decided, purportedly on the *voir dire*, were held to have adopted the correct course, even if only by accident, because the hearing of the issue as to admissibility was not in truth a trial within a trial at all: *F. (an infant)* v. *Chief Constable of Kent* [1982] Crim.L.R. 682 (D.C.).

There is no obligation on the accused to insist that the jury be excluded from the court when the admissibility of evidence is challenged, even if that challenge could properly have been heard on the *voir dire*: *R.* v. *Airey* [1985] Crim.L.R. 305 (C.A.).

5.—Law and Fact

1–24 Add Note 17a. See Mureinik, "The Application of Rules: Law or Fact" (1982) 98 L.Q.R. 587.

Fact

1–30 Note 69. The question of whether or not the jury are entitled to take into account the accused's own view of whether or not his conduct was honest, has been further confused by two decisions of the Court of Appeal in *R.* v. *McIvor* [1982] 1 W.L.R. 409 (C.A.) and *R.* v. *Ghosh* [1982] 3 W.L.R. 110. The court noted, and perhaps exaggerated, the conflict between such cases as *R.* v. *Boggeln* (see text), *R.* v. *Gilks* [1982] 1 W.L.R. 1341 (C.A.) and *R.* v. *Landy* [1981] 1 W.L.R. 409 (C.A.) (all cases where the subjectivist line was or appeared to be approved) and the more orthodox view expressed in *R.* v. *Feely* and *R.* v. *Greenstein* (see text) that it is the jury's view of what is dishonest and not the accused's which is relevant to the issue of criminal liability. In *R.* v. *McIvor* (above), the Court of Appeal restated the proposition that dishonesty was a question for the jury alone, but they appeared to draw a distinction between offences involving theft and those involving fraud, a distinction inconsistent with *R.* v. *Greenstein* (above). In *R.* v. *Ghosh* (above) the court removed this distinction, and brought back the accused's view of his own acts as being directly relevant to the question of whether or not he should be convicted of an offence of dishonesty. This does not, as some commentators have suggested, give the accused a double-barrelled attack on the indictment, entitling him to an acquittal if *either* the jury *or* he himself believed that the act with which he was charged was not a dishonest one. For these purposes the Court of Appeal took the question to be not the simple one of whether the accused thought that he was acting honestly, but whether he thought that *others* would think so. This is not dissimilar to the approach proposed in the main work; and while we recognise that it has the disadvantages as well as the advantages of sophistication, we do not think that the question is or could be a simple one, and respectfully suggest that the approach of the Court of Appeal in *R.* v. *Ghosh* is to be welcomed. (This view is not universally shared: see Dishonesty: the Objections to *Feely* and *Ghosh*—Edward Griew [1985] Crim.L.R. 341.)

CHAPTER 2.—MATTERS OF WHICH EVIDENCE IS UNNECESSARY

2.—Judicial Notice

(g) *Notorious facts*

2–21 Note 98. Judicial notice may be taken of the fact that the standard form of Lloyd's S.G. Policy, with appropriate Institute Warranties attached, is used worldwide: *Amin Rasheed Shipping Corp.* v. *Kuwait Insurance Co.* [1984] A.C. 50 (H.L.), *per* Lord Diplock at 64.5.

Add Note 99a. In the interests of uniformity, judicial notice will be taken of the fact that a flick-knife is an offensive weapon: *Gibson* v. *Wales* [1983] 1 W.L.R. 393 (D.C.); *R.* v. *Simpson* [1983] 1 W.L.R. 1494 (C.A.). The same considerations do not apply to sheath knives, where it is a question of fact in each case whether any particular sheath knife was an offensive weapon: *R.* v. *Williamson* (1977) 67 Cr.App.R. 15 (C.A.).

Note 2. Add *Waring* v. *Administração Geral* [1983] 1 Lloyd's Rep. 45: arbitrators may use their general knowledge of the relevant trade without putting the matters on which they rely to the parties. If, however, they have particular knowledge of the events which are the subject-matter of the dispute before them, they are bound to tell the parties of that knowledge so as to enable them to call evidence in order to support or contradict the arbitrators' understanding of the facts.

CHAPTER 4.—BURDEN AND STANDARD OF PROOF

1.—Burden of Proof

B. Meaning and Scope of Rule

(2) The evidential burden

(b) *The evidential burden in criminal cases*

4–10 If there is evidence of facts which could give rise to a defence of lawful excuse in a case of threatening to kill (Offences Against the Person Act 1861, s.16 as amended by Sched. 12 to the Criminal Law Act 1977) the onus lies with the prosecution to prove the absence of lawful excuse: *Cousins* [1982] Q.B. 526 (C.A.).

If in a case of handling stolen goods a defendant says that he believes that the goods are stolen, the prosecution is not relieved of proving that the goods *are* stolen: *R.* v. *De Acetis, The Times*, January 22, 1982.

4–13 The judge should only leave to the jury a defence which has not been put forward by the defendant when there was evidence from which the jury could reasonably infer that the defendant acted in a way which provided a defence at law. There was no duty to leave to the jury fanciful or speculative defences: *Critchley* (1982) Crim.L.R. 524, (C.A.) (A case of murder in which a defence of self-defence was raised for the first time in the defence speech. The Court of Appeal upheld the judge's direction that self-defence was not in issue.) The failure of a judge to leave a defence raised by evidence (no matter from what source) can amount to such a non-direction as to destroy the conviction if the Court of Appeal conclude that he was called upon to leave the defence to the jury: *R.* v. *Bashir* (1982) 77 Cr.App.R. 59, 62 (*per* Watkins L.J.)

Note 63. (i) *Non-insane Automatism*: Add *R.* v. *Stripp* (1978) 69 Cr.App.R. 318 (C.A.). (viii)(a) *Road Traffic Act* 1972. The provisions in Sched. 8 to the Transport Act 1981 have been substituted for ss.6–12 of the Road Traffic Act 1972.

Statutory and common law exceptions

(a) *Where a statute expressly casts the burden upon the defendant*

4–14 Where a burden of disproving a presumption is placed by statute on the defendant, he may discharge that burden by evidence elicited in cross-examination of prosecution witnesses: *R.* v. *Grant (Thomas)* [1985] Crim.L.R. 387.

NOTE 68. (i) *Diminished Responsibility*: Add: While medical evidence is not in terms required by the Homicide Act 1957, s.2(1), in order to establish diminished responsibility, it is a practical necessity if the defence is to be run at all: *R.* v. *Dix* (1982) 74 Cr.App.R. 306, (C.A.), applying *R.* v. *Byrne* [1960] 2 Q.B. 596, 44 Cr.App.R. 246.

(iv) *Prevention of Corruption Act 1916*, s.2. Add *R.* v. *Braithwaite* [1983] 1 W.L.R. 385; [1983] 2 All E.R. 87; 77 Cr.App.R. 34.

(xiv) *Sexual Offences Act*, 1956, ss.30(2); *R.* v. *Grant (Thomas), ante.*

(xv) *Road Traffic Act*, 1972, s.10(2), as substituted by Schedule 8 of the Transport Act, 1981. Once the defendant admitted driving his car on the day in question and once the sample of breath showed an excess of alcohol, section 10(2) operated to transfer the burden to the defendant to show that he consumed alcohol after he ceased to drive: *Patterson* v. *Charlton* [1986] R.T.R. 18.

(b) *Where a statute creates an offence subject to exceptions, provisos, etc.*

4–16 (ii) TRIALS ON INDICTMENT. The principle in *R.* v. *Edwards* [1975] Q.B. 27; (1974) 59 Cr.App.R. 213 has been extended in *R.* v. *Hunt* [1986] 1 All E.R. 184 (C.A.). In *Edwards*, Lawton L.J. limited the exception to the fundamental rule that the prosecution must prove every element of the offence charged to "offences arising under enactments which prohibit the doing of an act save in specified circumstances or by persons of specified classes or with specified qualifications or with the licence or permission of specified authorities." In *Hunt*, the defendant was charged with unlawful possession of morphine, contrary to the Misuse of Drugs Act 1971, s.5(2). By Regulations, section 5 did not have effect in relation to a preparation containing not more than 0.2 per cent. of morphine. The Court of Appeal held that a persuasive burden rested on the defendant to bring himself within the exception created by the Regulations. It is suggested, cogently, in [1986] Crim.L.R. at page 175 that *Hunt* can be regarded as an example of a principle already established in *Edwards* that what is now section 101 of the Magistrates Courts Act 1980 states the common law when it places on the defendant the onus of proving exemptions, exceptions, etc.

Should the persuasive burden be upon the defendant in a criminal case?

4–18 In *Hunt, ante*, the Court of Appeal noted academic criticism of inroads into *Woolmington* v. *D.P.P.* [1935] A.C. 462, but followed *Edwards* in casting the persuasive burden on the defendant.

2.—STANDARD OF PROOF

(1) Criminal cases

4–31 The failure of the judge to direct the jury was a serious defect in the summing-up which could not be cured by the fact that prosecuting and defence counsel referred to the standard of proof in their speeches and by the fact that the jury was experienced: *R.* v. *Edwards* (1983) 77 Cr.App.R. 5 (C.A.). The judge's duty is "to direct the jury on the standard of proof so as to ensure that the direction was heard by them in each criminal trial with the authority which only the judge could give to such a direction": *Edwards, supra*, p. 7.

In *Edwards* the court said that the proviso could be applied in cases where there had been a failure to direct the jury on the burden of proof, as in any other case. The court found that the case against the appellant was overwhelming and applied the proviso, although there had been no direction as to the standard of proof.

NOTE 39. Add: A direction to the jury that they must be satisfied so that they are "reasonably sure" is enough to vitiate a subsequent correct direction as to the standard of proof: *R.* v. *Sweeney, The Times*, October 22, 1983 (C.A.).

(c) *Admissibility of evidence*

4–34 In *R.* v. *Ewing* [1983] Q.B. 1039; [1983] 3 W.L.R. 1, a differently constituted Court of Appeal said that the reasoning in the judgment in *Angeli* was *per incuriam*. The court held that in a criminal trial where handwriting is to be used for the purposes of comparison under section 8 of the Criminal Procedure Act 1865, it should be proved to the satisfaction of the judge to be genuine and the standard of proof should be the normal criminal standard.

The Court's reasoning was as follows:

(i) Section 8 of the 1865 Act says nothing about the standard of proof to be used.

(ii) The standard of proof is governed by the common law (see *Blyth* v. *Blyth* (No. 2) [1966] A.C. 643 (H.L.), to which the court in *Angeli* had not been referred).

(iii) Therefore in civil cases, the civil standards should be used; and in criminal cases, the criminal standard.

This view is consistent with the view expressed in the main text. It is submitted that *Ewing* should be followed in preference to *Angeli*.

(2) Civil cases

4–35 (a) *Generally*. In *Khawaja* v. *Secretary of State for the Home Department* [1984] A.C. 74, the House of Lords considered the standard of proof in an immigration case involving the liberty of the person. It was held, approving *Bater* v. *Bater* [1951] P. 35, *Re Dellow's Will Trusts* [1964] 1 W.L.R. 451 and *Hornal* v. *Neuberger Products Ltd.* [1957] 1 Q.B. 247, that the executive must justify the detention on a preponderance of probability. Lord Scarman said, at page 113, "The flexibility of the civil standard of proof suffices to ensure that the court will require the high probability which is appropriate to what is at stake."

On a trial of a defamation action by a jury, it is not generally necessary for the judge to direct the jury as to the flexibility of the civil standard of proof according to the seriousness of the alleged defamatory statement; in most cases it is a matter for the jury's common sense: *Lawrence* v. *Chester Chronicle, The Times*, February 8, 1986 (C.A.).

4–36 (b) *Proof of criminal offences in civil proceedings*. Where a complaint of a criminal offence by a police officer did not result in a prosecution because the D.P.P. considered the evidence insufficient for criminal proceedings, disciplinary proceedings on the same grounds were held to be permissible, although McNeill J. held that the criminal standard of proof would apply in the disciplinary tribunal: *R.* v. *Police Complaints Board, ex parte Madden* [1983] 1 W.L.R. 447; [1983] 2 All E.R. 353. However, the Court of Appeal in *R.* v. *Hampshire County Council, ex parte Ellerton* [1985] 1 W.L.R. 749; [1985] 1 All E.R. 599, doubted the correctness of McNeill J.'s view. In *Ellerton* it was held that although the Fire Services (Discipline) Regulations, 1948, were drafted in the language of the criminal law, the civil standard of proof applied in the disciplinary proceedings. See also *Saeed* v. *G.L.C. (I.L.E.A.)* [1986] I.R.L.R. 23 (Popplewell J.) (disciplinary proceedings against a school keeper).

CHAPTER 5.—THE BEST EVIDENCE RULE

Its present scope: strict proof not generally necessary

5–04 *Kajala* v. *Noble* is now reported in (1982) 74 Cr.App.R. 149.

Exceptions

5–06 Care must be taken in admitting copies of documents if admissibility may be in question and the defendant is unrepresented: *R.* v. *Wayte* (1983) 76 Cr.App.R. 110 (C.A.).

The Report of the Fraud Trials Committee (the Roskill Report), 1986, proposes that in fraud trials the judge should have a general power to order that a copy document should be admissible to the same extent as the original: paragraph 5.40.

CHAPTER 7.—THE FACT OR TRANSACTION IN ISSUE

2.—Physical Conditions, Emotions Opinion and State of Mind

(b) *Declarations Out of Court*

7–41 *As to knowledge.* In *Blastland* [1985] 3 W.L.R. 345 the House of Lords emphasised that the principle that evidence may be admitted to prove the maker's knowledge in state of mind can only apply when the state of mind evidenced by the statement is either itself directly in issue at the trial or is of direct and immediate relevance to an issue which arises at the trial.

In *Blastland* the defendant was charged with the murder of a boy, K. The defence was that another man, M, had murdered B. At the trial the judge refused to allow the defence to call certain witnesses to prove that M had said (at a time before the boy's body had been found) that a boy had been murdered. The House of Lords held that the evidence had rightly been excluded because M's knowledge of the murder was neither in issue at the trial nor was it relevant to the issue at the trial i.e. whether B had murdered K, Lord Bridge (in a speech with which the other members of the House concurred) said:— "[The] admissibility of a statement tendered in evidence as proof of the maker's knowledge or other state of mind must always depend on the degree of relevence of the state of mind sought to be proved to the issue in relation to which the evidence is tendered". (p. 358).

CHAPTER 8.—AGENCY, PARTNERSHIP, COMPANIES, COMMON PURPOSE

4.—Acts and Declarations in Pursuance of a Common Purpose

Common purpose

8–15 See also *R.* v. *Donat* (1986) 82 Cr.App.R. 173 (C.A.).

CHAPTER 9.—FACTS RELEVANT TO PROVE THE MAIN FACT

3.—Course of Business

9–22 *R.* v. *Asif* [1985] Crim.L.R. 679 (C.A.) was an example of a case in which evidence of transactions prior to the period covered by the indictment "to set the overall context of the course of the defendant's business" was admissible (V.A.T. offences under the Finance Act 1972).

PHIPSON PARAGRAPH

5.—STANDARDS OF COMPARISON

Handwriting

9–42 NOTE 22. *R.* v. *Angeli* has been overruled by *R.* v. *Ewing* [1983] Q.B. 1039 (C.A.): see below § 27–67.

CHAPTER 10.—FACTS RELEVANT TO SHOW IDENTITY, OR CONNECT THE PARTIES WITH THE TRANSACTION

Personal characteristics, etc.

10–01 As to visual identification and identification by photographs, see *post*, § 27–61 *et seq*.

As to directions to a jury in identification cases, see *post*, § 32–15.

Previous conduct, motive, capacity, attempts, threats, enmity, opportunity

10–02 NOTE 20. The dicta in *R.* v. *Ball* [1911] A.C. 47, 68, were criticised in *R.* v. *Berry* [1986] Crim.L.R. 394 (C.A.); see *post*, § 11–12, 11–16.

Fingerprints. Footmarks

10–10 The Criminal Justice Act 1967, s.33 and the Magistrates' Courts Act 1980, s.49 have been repealed. The statutory provisions relating to the taking of fingerprints are now in the Police and Criminal Evidence Act 1984, ss.27, 61, 64 and 65. The following is a short summary:

(i) Fingerprints include palm prints: s.65.

(ii) Fingerprints may be taken with the consent of the person concerned (or where appropriate, their parent or guardian): ss.61(1), (2), 65.

(iii) Fingerprints may be taken without consent from a person detained at a police station after he is charged or informed that he will be reported: s.61(3)(b).

(iv) There is provision for authorisation of the taking of fingerprints from a detained person without consent before charge for the purposes of the inquiry: s.61(3)(a), (4), (5).

(v) There is provision for the taking of fingerprints without consent from certain convicted persons: s.61(6). Attendance at a police station may be required for that purpose: s.27.

(vi) Fingerprints of those acquitted are to be destroyed: s.64.

(vii) Various procedural safeguards are set out in section 61. See also Code of Practice for the Identification of Persons by Police Officers (issued under section 66 of the Act), paragraphs 3.1 to 3.6. Reasonable force may be used to take fingerprints: s.117.

See also article by Donald Campbell, Fingerprints: A Review [1985] Crim.L.R. on the practical aspects of fingerprint evidence.

Tracker dogs

10–12 See article by Gerard McCormack, The Admissibility of Tracker Dog Evidence [1985] Crim.L.R. 202. In accordance with the article's conclusions on authorities in other jurisdictions, it is clear that such evidence is in principle admissible.

Blood tests. Body samples of other kinds

10–13 The Police and Criminal Evidence Act 1984 enacts detailed provisions for the taking of "intimate" samples (including samples of blood) and "non-intimate" samples: ss.62 to 65. The following is a short summary:

(i) Intimate samples are defined by section 65 and include samples of blood and other body fluids.

(ii) Non-intimate samples, also defined by section 65, include head hair samples and footprints.

(iii) Samples of either kind may be taken only with the consent of the person (or where appropriate, their parent or guardian) or in certain limited circumstances on the authorisation of a police officer of the rank of at least superintendent: ss.62(1) to (6), 63(1) to (6).

(iv) Most kinds of intimate sample may be taken only by a registered medical practitioner: section 62(9).

(v) Reasonable force may be used to take non-intimate samples: section 117.

(vi) It appears that force may not be used to take intimate samples, even where a registered medical practitioner is not involved, but if consent is refused, then

(a) a court may draw such inferences from the refusal as appear proper; and

(b) the refusal may, on the basis of such inferences, be treated as, or as capable of amounting to, corroboration of any evidence against the person in relation to which the refusal is material: s.62(10).

(vii) Various procedural safeguards are set out in sections 62 and 63. See also Code of Practice for the Identification of Persons by Police Officers, *ante*, paragraphs 5.1 to 5.12.

(viii) Samples of those acquitted are to be destroyed: section 64.

10–15 See also the Blood Tests (Evidence of Paternity) Regulations 1971, S.I. 1971 No. 1861, as amended. These regulations govern the procedure for taking blood tests in cases before the High Court and the county court.

CHAPTER 11.—FACTS RELEVANT TO PROVE STATES OF MIND

2.—Intention

When in issue, or relevant

11–12 In *R.* v. *Berry* [1986] Crim.L.R. 394 (C.A.) the defendant was charged with murder. His defence *inter alia*, was that the act was accidental and that he lacked the necessary intent. It was held that the judge was wrong to admit evidence of past incidents (including past words) of the defendant to prove the intent at the time death was caused. Such evidence should not, generally speaking, be permitted. "What is relevant is evidence of what was said or done at the time or at a time close or relatively close to the act."

The court criticised dicta of Lord Atkinson in *R.* v. *Ball* [1911] A.C. 47 at p. 68; see § 10–12, Note 20. It is submitted that Lord Atkinson's dicta remain a correct expression of general principle. However, the application of the principle may differ in cases where intention is in issue from cases in which the issue is whether the defendant committed the crime. And in the former type of case a careful distinction between motive and intention may lead the court either to decide that the evidence is too remote in time and hence of no probative value or to exclude the evidence as more prejudicial than probative.

3.—Motive

11–16 See also *R.* v. *Berry, ante.*

CHAPTER 12.—SIMILAR FACTS

A.—General Principles

12–01 Similar fact evidence may be admissible to establish that the defendant was the person who committed the offence even when the evidence is of previous conduct which was not criminal. In *R.* v. *Butler, The Times*, June 24, 1986 (C.A.), it was held that evidence of previous sexual behaviour of the defendant with his former girl friend, with her consent, was admissible of charges of indecent assault and rape on other women because that behaviour bore a striking similarity to conduct during the commission of the offences. The Court of Appeal pointed out that when it came to the exercise of discretion, evidence of previous behaviour that was not criminal was likely to be less prejudicial than evidence of previous criminal behaviour.

Discretion of court

12–06 In *R.* v. *Rimmer and Beech* [1983] Crim.L.R. 250, the defendants were charged with murder. Each blamed the other. Counsel for one defendant cross-examined the second defendant as to the latter's mental health. The second defendant sought leave to call evidence on this issue. The judge refused leave. The Court of Appeal upheld this decision since to open up such issues would involve an inordinately long examination as to the man's mental health and would have blurred the crucial issues for the jury. The Court apparently considered that, beside the problem of opening up side issues which might confuse the jury, the evidence was insufficiently relevant. This is however not clear from the report.

B.—In Criminal Cases—Evidence for the Prosecution

The test of admissibility: striking similarity

12–10 The test of "striking similarity" was reaffirmed by the Court of Appeal in *R.* v. *Dowell* (1983) 147 J.P.N. 829. The court approved the summary of the law in *Cross on Evidence* (5th ed.) p. 202.

Need a specific defence be raised before similar fact evidence is admitted?

12–20 In *R.* v. *Lewis* (1982) 76 Cr.App.R. 33 the defendant was indicted for offences of indecency against children. Four incidents were involved. In the case of three of the incidents, the defence was accident or that there was an innocent explanation. In the fourth case, the defendant denied that the incident had occurred at all. Evidence was admitted (a) of documents obtained from the Paedophilic Society and (b) of the defendant's references to himself as a paedophile. The defendant appealed against his conviction on the grounds that:

(i) where there is substantial dispute as to whether the acts complained of took place, the prosecution is not entitled to put forward evidence designed to negative accident or an innocent explanation of the acts,

(ii) the judge should have excluded the evidence as a matter of discretion.

The Court of Appeal held that:

(i) The evidence of paedophilia was admissible as to those incidents where the defence was accident or innocent explanation and the fact that it was inadmissible on the count when the incident was denied did not render the evidence inadmissible in the context of the other counts.

(ii) The evidence could have an unduly prejudicial effect if its true impact and significance was not carefully explained to the jury. But since the judge had done this the appeal did not succeed on that ground either.

Proving similar facts

12–32 Where the defence involved casting serious imputations on the character of a prosecution witness, the Court of Appeal held that the judge had properly allowed the prosecution to adduce similar fact evidence as additional evidence: *R.* v. *Hill* [1982] Crim.L.R. 518.

12–34 *Mechanical agents and instruments.* The test record print-out of an automatic breath-testing device is admissible as evidence, since the print-out constitutes the product of a mechanical device which, at common law, falls into the category of real evidence: *Castle* v. *Cross* [1985] 1 W.L.R. 1372. See further, § 16–11.

To prove guilty knowledge in cases of handling stolen goods

12–55 The reasoning of the final sentence of the text has been proved correct by the decision of the Court of Appeal in *R.* v. *Perry* [1984] Crim.L.R. 680. The court held, allowing the appeal against conviction, that, if a judge came to the conclusion that, although the evidence was admissible, the circumstances were such that it really could be of minimal assistance to the jury, then, notwithstanding section 27(3), it must be his duty to exclude the evidence. The Court of Appeal has again emphasized in *R.* v. *Rasini, The Times*, March 20, 1986, that evidence should not be adduced under section 27(3)(b) as a matter of course; the court has a discretion to admit such evidence when the demands of justice warrant it.

In *R.* v. *Simmons* [1986] Crim.L.R. 397 (C.A.), the court pointed out that section 27(3)(a) can be applied separately from section 27(1)(b).

C.—In Civil Cases

(a) *The Principle of Admissibility*

12–59 Note 39. Add: followed in *Berger* v. *Raymond Sun Limited* [1984] 1 W.L.R. 625.

Note 42. Add: distinguished in *Berger* v. *Raymond Sun Limited* (*supra*) as turning on its particular facts. In *Berger* the evidence of a handwriting expert to prove previous forgeries was held admissible. By pleading that he would only have signed with authority, the defendant put in issue his normal conduct, and what he did on other occasions became relevant not only in respect of signing his mother's name but also in respect of signing for other members of his family.

(b) *Principle of Exclusion*

12–62 Note 46: After *Metropolitan Asylum* v. *Hill*, 47 L.T. 29, add: considered in *Berger* (*ante*) at 632 C–F, where Warner J. stated that the court should take into consideration the probable probative value of the evidence sought to be adduced, and the extent to which its introduction would complicate and prolong the trial.

Existence or occurrence of the main fact

12–67 *Mechanical agents and instruments: engines, etc.* See also *Castle* v. *Cross* [1985] 1 All E.R. 87, *ante*, § 12–34.

CHAPTER 13.—CHARACTER

4.—Evidence of the Character of the Accused

(2) Good character of the accused

(a) *Evidence of witnesses other than the accused*

13–10 Note 37. Add to footnote *R.* v. *Doosti* (1985) 82 Cr.App.R. 181 (C.A.). Evidence of a previous acquittal on a *similar* charge (of supplying prohibited drugs) was held inadmissible in chief because it was held to be relevant to no issue in the case. It must be that this was because the mere fact of the acquittal did not amount to evidence of good character. (The principal reason the accused sought to adduce the evidence was, it appears, to discredit the police officer who prosecuted him in respect of both offences: it would be inadmissible for that purpose—see text at § 13–05. Evidence of the acquittal was however permitted to be brought out in re-examination: see below § 13–47A.)

(3) Evidence of the bad character of the accused

13–16 Note 78. Add: *R.* v. *Nye* (1982) 75 Cr.App.R. 247 (C.A.), where the accused in a criminal case has a conviction which is "spent" under the Rehabilitation of Offenders Act 1974, a direction should be sought from the judge at the outset of the trial as to whether or not the accused may be treated as a man of good character. The matter is one for the discretion of the trial judge, and he should take into account how long ago the conviction became spent and how dissimilar to the present charge is the offence of which the accused was formerly convicted.

(d) *Cross-examination of the accused as to character*

13–24 Note 11. Add: *R.* v. *Palmer* [1983] Crim.L.R. 252 (C.A.), (no cross-examination about acquittals—see further below § 13–47).

Exceptions to section 1(f)

13–25 Notes 13–14. In *R.* v. *Weekes* [1983] Crim.L.R. 801 (C.A.), the accused pleaded guilty to certain charges as to which he had made admissions in a statement to the police. He pleaded not guilty to other charges, the subject of a separate indictment and said that admissions in the statement relating to those offences had been obtained by intimidation. The trial judge permitted the prosecution to cross-examine him about the charges to which he had pleaded guilty, for the purpose of showing consistency on the part of the prosecution witnesses. *Held* that, even though the cross-examination might have been permitted under section 1(*f*)(ii), the conviction would be quashed because there was no right to introduce the convictions under section 1(*f*)(i) for the stated purpose. See also Tapper, *The Meaning of Section 1(f)(i) of the Criminal Evidence Act 1898* in Tapper (Ed.) *Crime Proof and Punishment* (1981); Pattenden, *The Purpose of Cross-Examination under Section 1(f) of the Criminal Evidence Act 1898* [1982] Crim.L.R. 707.

13–26 Add at the end: for a discussion of the purposes for which cross-examination under section 1(*f*)(i) is permissible, see Pattenden, "The Purpose of Cross-examination Under Section 1(f) of the Criminal Evidence Act 1898," [1982] Crim.L.R. 707.

General effect of section 1(f)(ii)

13–29 Note 34. Add: *R.* v. *de Vere* [1981] 3 W.L.R. 593 (C.A.), where it was held: (a) that, an unsworn statement attacking the prosecution witnesses does not expose the accused to cross-examination under section 1(*f*)(ii); (b) that, following *Gadbury* and *Campbell* (see text), an assertion of his good character given by the accused in the course of an unsworn statement may be the subject of evidence in rebuttal, subject to the leave of the court being first obtained. The consistency of the two halves of this decision is less than striking.

Operation of section 1(f)(ii)

13–37 Add at Notes 70–78 *R.* v. *Britzman* (1982) 76 Cr.App.R. 134 (C.A.), is of general importance in relation to the application of the "imputations" provisions of section 1(*f*)(ii). It was held that merely to deny admissions alleged by the police to have been made to them or in their presence would, on the facts of that case, suffice to deprive the accused of his protection under section 1(*f*), even though his counsel was astute enough to avoid the suggestion that the police were guilty of perjury. The decision in *R.* v. *M'Gee and Cassidy* (see text) was preferred to that in *R.* v. *Nelson* (criticised *ibid.*). The court, in laying down guidelines for the application of section 1(*f*)(ii), reiterated the well-established principle that a mere emphatic denial of a charge would not justify cross-examination on the accused's record, and it was observed in particular, that a denial of a particular statement was not the same as the suggestion that the account of the whole of an interview was fabricated. Similarly, the court issued a reminder that it must be recognised that defendants sometimes use wild language in giving evidence, and that that will not necessarily involve the casting of imputations on the character of prosecution witnesses, especially where the form of cross-examination to which the accused has been subjected has in effect trapped him into an intemperate observation. Finally, the court observed that it was unnecessary to rely on the section when the other evidence against the accused is overwhelming, although we have doubts as to the appropriateness of the trial judge being required to make an assessment of the evidence, especially when it is incomplete, for the purpose of guessing how it will appear to a jury. Nor is the rationale of this limitation very obvious.

The decision in *R.* v. *St. Louis* (1984) 79 Cr.App.R. 53 (C.A.) has reaffirmed that "a mere emphatic denial" will not result in the loss of the accused shield. In going back to *R.* v. *Clark* (1955) 39 Cr.App.R. 120 (C.C.A.) as the *locus classicus* for the exposition of this principle, the Court of Appeal to some extent qualifies *R.* v. *Britzmann*: but it is thought that the propositions stated above remain sound.

Purpose of cross-examination under section 1(f)(ii)

13–41 Note 90. Add: Pattenden *op. cit.* § 13–25 above; *Reflections on the Criminal Evidence Act 1898*, R. J. C. Munday [1985] 49 C.L.J. 62; *Stepping Beyond the Bounds of Credibility: the Application of Section 1(f)(ii) of the Criminal Evidence Act 1898*, Roderick Munday [1986] Crim.L.R. 511. The theme of Munday's articles is that there is no justification for a unitary view of character in general or veracity in particular, and that the distinction between evidence relevant to the issue and evidence going to credibility is artificial and unreal in the context of the accused's convictions.

Indivisibility of character of accused

13–43 NOTES 2–5. See *R.* v. *Watts* (1983) 77 Cr.App.R. 126 (C.A.) (considered below, § 13–45 n. 20). On the validity of the hypothesis that character is indivisible, see R. J. C. Munday, *Reflections on the Criminal Evidence Act 1898* [1985] C.L.J. 62, where it is pointed out that even dishonesty (as compared with other moral or legal failings) is not a seamless web.

The principle that the accused's character is indivisible can permit the latter to adduce evidence in rebuttal of evidence of bad character put to him in cross-examination: *R.* v. *Doosti* (1985) 82 Cr.App.R. 181 (C.A.). This is so even if the evidence could not have been led by the accused in chief.

NOTE 8. Add: In both *R.* v. *Stubbs* (1981) 79 Cr.App.R. 246 (C.A.) and *R.* v. *Winter* [1980] Crim.L.R. 659 (C.A.), it was held that an accused ought not to be cross-examined as to credit, after he had thrown away his shield, on the basis that the entries in his application for legal aid were false.

13–45 NOTE 20. Add: *R.* v. *Watts* (1983) 77 Cr.App.R. 126 (C.A.). In this case, the Court of Appeal gave effect to some of the criticisms levelled at the decision in *R.* v. *France*, which was said to have been misreported and suspect. In *R.* v. *Watts* the accused, a man of low intelligence, with two previous convictions for indecently assaulting small children, was accused of an indecent assault against a woman which had taken place near his home. He alleged the admissions which he was said to have made to the police were fabricated, and his conviction was quashed on the ground that the trial judge had erred in permitting his previous convictions to be put to him in cross-examination under section 1(*f*)(ii). It must be said that the decision has not rendered the law any clearer or more certain, because the ground on which the Court of Appeal proceeded was that the trial judge had exercised his discretion in the wrong way, and that neither *R.* v. *France* nor *R.* v. *Duncalf* (see text) gave guidance on the exercise of the discretion. Nor is the question of the correct principles governing the exercise of the discretion satisfactorily resolved by the latest decision (although we think that it has much to commend it), because there was not a full consideration of the relevant authorities: see further below § 13–49.

13–46 NOTE 21. In *R.* v. *Rowson* [1985] 2 All E.R. 539 (1984), 80 Cr.App.R. 218 (C.A.), it was the view of the court that cross-examination under section 1(f)(ii) is permissible at the instance of the co-accused. This is consistent with the approach of the Court in *R.* v. *Lovett*; but dicta in the later case go much further. Indeed, it was said that *R.* v. *Lovett* was exceptional and confined to its own facts so far as it suggested that the Court might have a discretion to prevent cross-examination of one accused by another when the former has thrown away his shield by casting imputations on the prosecution. The overriding principle which it was said could be discovered from *Murdoch* v. *Taylor* [1965] A.C. 574 (H.L.) was that *all* admissible evidence should be available to an accused, even if that is to the prejudice of a co-accused. The dicta in *Lovett* were said to have been influenced by the form which section 1(f)(iii) then took. While this latter point may be true, it is surely *Murdoch* v. *Taylor* which is exceptional in depriving a trial judge of any right to exercise discretionary control over the admissibility of evidence in one particular respect. There is reason for such a restriction where section 1(f)(iii) is concerned, and for these purposes it makes no differences whether one is considering the amended or unamended version of that provision. In that case the evidence which triggers the admissibility of the relevant defendant's criminal record consists of evidence given against another person charged in the same proceedings. The position is different under section 1(f)(ii) where an attack may not affect the co-accused at all; it may very well not prejudice him; and in some cases, it may redound to his advantage. It is hard to see, in any of these cases, that it would be right that a judge is constrained to permit the co-accused to conduct a cross-examination on the other defendant's record. This would be particularly unjust in a case where the circumstances were such that a trial judge would not conceivably exercise his discretion in such a way as to permit the prosecution to do so. The dicta on this point were necessary for neither of the decisions of the Court of Appeal, and we respectfully prefer the reasoning of the earlier decision on this point.

Procedural aspects of section 1(f)(ii)

13–47 NOTE 31. Add: This makes it desirable that the judge knows in advance of the defendant's character: *R.* v. *Ewing* [1983] Q.B. 1039 (C.A.). The position is different in the case of magistrates, who also act as triers of fact—see *R.* v. *Liverpool City Justices, ex p. Topping* [1983] 1 W.L.R. 119 (D.C.).

Add NOTE 32a. See *R.* v. *Palmer* [1983] Crim.L.R. 252 (C.A.), where an accused referred to his previous convictions for the purpose of showing that he had always pleaded guilty to offences of which he was guilty. In the course of cross-examination as to whether or not juries had always believed him, the accused said that he had been acquitted by a jury when he had pleaded not guilty. The judge refused an application which was immediately made on behalf of the accused that he discharge the jury, but he warned them to disregard the answer and the acquittal, without recurring to this in his summing-up. It was *held* that the accused had put his bad character in issue, and that in those circumstances counsel had to be particularly careful; but that the trial judge had acted perfectly properly. It was said that it might have been different if the accused had put his *good* character in issue. It is, with respect, hard to see (a) how the accused's bad character was "in issue," since there was no dispute about it, and the accused was himself relying on it; (b) how the acquittal reflected on the accused's character, when all it did in fact was to lend credence to his case that he pleaded guilty when he was guilty; and (c) how proviso (ii) to section 1(*f*) ever came to be relevant at all, because, the accused's bad character having been "revealed," the prohibition never bit in the first place: see *Jones* v. *D.P.P.* (Text § 13–25 to § 13–26). As it is not uncommon for an accused to rely positively on his previous convictions, the implications of the decision in *R.* v. *Palmer* may require that it be reconsidered.

Judicial discretion under section 1(f)(ii)

NOTE 35a. This is a discretion which the judge cannot simply ignore: he must consider whether or not to exercise it. So, if he admits evidence of bad character, erroneously believing it to be admissible on the issue of credibility without the benefit of the statute, the ensuing conviction is liable to be quashed even though the evidence *might* have been introduced pursuant to section 1(f)(ii): *R.* v. *Weekes* (1983) 77 Cr.App.R. 207 (C.A.).

13–47A *R.* v. *Doosti* (1985) 82 Cr.App.R. 181 (C.A.) is an isolated illustration of evidence being elicited in re-examination in rebuttal of the prosecutor's cross-examination as to bad character: see above § 13–43 notes 2–5.

13–48 NOTE 40. Add: *R.* v. *Nye* (1982) 75 Cr.App.R. 247 (C.A.), shows that when exercising the discretion under section 1(*f*)(ii) the judge should take into account the provisions of the Rehabilitation of Offenders Act 1974.

13–49 Add: *R.* v. *Watts* (*supra* § 13–45 n. 20). The Court of Appeal held that the two convictions for indecently assaulting small children had little, if any, relevance to credibility, not being offences of dishonesty. While, as stated above, there is much to be said for this approach, consistent as it is with the dicta in *Maxwell* v. *D.P.P.* [1935] A.C. 309 (H.L.) (on which the Court of Appeal expressly relied) as to the danger of the jury confusing matters directly relevant to the issue of guilt and those which go merely to credibility, no reference was made to the indivisibility of the accused's character (see text § 13–43) nor to the procedure following in *Selvey* v. *D.P.P.* (see text § 13–45, n. 15) where convictions for dishonesty were excluded, and convictions for similar sexual offences were permitted to be the subject of cross-examination. We think, with respect, that the approach adopted in *R.* v. *Watts* was the right one; but the Court of Appeal first distinguished the decision in *R.* v. *Burke* (1985) 82 Cr.App.R. 156 (C.A.) and then disapproved it in *R.* v. *Powell* (1986) 82 Cr.App.R. 165 (C.A.). In both cases, attention was drawn to the fact that *D.P.P.* v. *Selvey* (see text) was not cited in *R.* v. *Watts*; and the indivisibility of the accused's character was re-assessed in *R.* v. *Powell*. It was in effect said that tit-for-tat was the correct way in which to apply section 1(*f*)(ii). (This would appear to circumscribe the judicial discretion very narrowly.)

NOTES 46–47. Add: *R.* v. *Varley* [1982] 2 All E.R. 519 (C.A.) lays down guidelines for the court's approach to section 1(*f*)(iii) of the 1898 Act. In that case, one of two defendants jointly charged with robbery alleged that his admitted participation was due to the threats of the other accused. The latter denied that he had taken part in the robbery at all, and alleged that his co-accused was lying. The Court of Appeal held that he had rightly been permitted to be cross-examined on his record under section 1(*f*)(iii), and stated the relevant principles as follows:

(a) The expression "evidence against any other person charged in the same proceedings" in the sub-paragraph means evidence which supports the prosecution case or undermines the defence of the other defendant.
(b) Once the subsection was applicable, there was no discretion to prevent cross-examination on behalf of the co-assured under it, though in appropriate cases there might be justification in allowing separation of trials.
(c) It was immaterial whether the evidence which triggered the operation of the subsection was given in chief or in cross-examination.
(d) A hostile intent was unnecessary to bring the subsection into operation: the test for its applicability was objective.
(e) Where the case fell within the category of undermining a co-defendant, a cautious approach was to be adopted: it is insufficient that the evidence of one accused is inconvenient for a co-accused, nor is mere inconsistency between their respective evidence of itself sufficient to activate the subsection.
(f) A mere denial that one accused took part in an alleged joint venture will not justify a cross-examination under section 1(*f*)(iii): the evidence must also point to the involvement of his co-accused.
(g) However, contradiction of the other defendant's account of the affair might well (as in the instant case) amount to "evidence against" that defendant.

The Court in this case suggested that it would be unnecessary thereafter to refer to any other authority for guidance on the application of section 1(*f*)(iii); and it certainly contains a most helpful summary of the applicable principles. Those who wish to look behind it all the same will find additional assistance in the cases of *R.* v. *Davis* and *R.* v. *Bruce* (to be found in the main work) and *R.* v. *Hatton* (1976) 64 Cr.App.R. 88 (C.A.), (which ought to be, but appears to have slipped through the net).

NOTE 49. Add: consideration of the different views of the Court of Appeal in *R.* v. *Lovett* and *R.* v. *Rowson* (see above, § 13–37) prompts the question: does the decision in *Murdoch* v. *Taylor* exclude the operation of the judicial discretion where accused A gives evidence against co-accused B, who regards it as bad tactics to introduce A's bad character, and who finds his decision subverted by co-accused C, who seek to exercise a right, allegedly untramelled by any judicial discretion, to cross-examine a man who has given no evidence against *him.* Section 1(*f*)(iii) was not intended for his benefit. No doubt the protection of co-defendants was not the only purpose of the proviso, but we think that it would be wrong if the discretion of the judge were ousted utterly in a case of this class.

The decision in *Murdoch* v. *Taylor* is not contrary to this view, and indeed in the leading speech, that of Lord Donovan, there are hints that the discretion has not been excluded in such a case as that here envisaged. He expressly recognizes an exclusionary discretion in the trial judge in the case where it is the prosecution who wishes to rely on section 1(f)(iii): p. 593. Moreover, in dealing with earlier authorities approved by him, Lord Donovan said (p. 590D–E) that they decided "that where proviso (f)(iii) applied, the trial judge had no discretion whether or not to allow questions to be put thereunder. The co-accused *who was affected* had a right to do so if he wished" [emphasis added]. We think that if the co-accused "who was not affected" wishes to take advantage of the strict words of the proviso, the judge has a discretion, and, in the appropriate circumstances may prohibit such a cross-examination.

13–51 Add: see Pattenden, *op. cit.* § 13–25 (*supra*).

5.—CHARACTER OF THIRD PARTIES

13–53 Add NOTE 55a. See generally *The Character of Victims and Third Parties in Criminal Proceedings Other than Rape Trials*, Rosemary Pattenden [1986] Crim.L.R. 367.

NOTE 62. Add: *R.* v. *Viola* [1982] 1 W.L.R. 1138 (C.A.). The decision in *R.* v. *Lawrence* and *R.* v. *Mills* were followed, save that a dictum in the latter case that it was a matter for a judge's discretion whether or not to allow the complainant in a prosecution for rape to be cross-examined on her sexual conduct on other occasions was disapproved. It was not a matter of "discretion," but of "judgment" (although we do not fully appreciate the distinction). In the instant case, it was held that the trial judge was right to refuse to allow cross-examination of the prosecutrix as to whether or not she had had intercourse with her boy-friend on the afternoon following the evening of the alleged rape, but wrong in refusing to allow cross-examination as to an alleged attempt by her to seduce two comparative strangers on that evening, or as to an all but naked man alleged to have been seen in her maisonette the next morning.

See Z. Adler, *Rape—The Intention of Parliament and the Practice of the Courts* (1982) 45 M.L.R. 664; D. W. Elliott, *Rape Complainants' Sexual Experi-*

ence with Third Parties [1984] Crim.L.R. 4; J. Temkin, *Regulating Sexual History Evidence—the Limits of Discretionary Registration* (1984) 33 I.C.L.Q. 942; Z. Adler, *The Relevance of Sexual History in Rape: Problems of Subjective Interpretation* [1985] Crim.L.R. 769.

Generally

13–59A If the character of a person other than an accused is relevant to an issue, subject to the exception of the prosecutrix in a case of rape, it may generally be proved. It is not very often that the character of a person with no connection with the trial is relevant to an issue before the jury, but in *R.* v. *Djerdet* [1984] Crim.L.R. 359 (C.A.), the accused was charged with being concerned with three others (A, B and C) in the importation of a consignment of heroin, his defence being that he thought that he was participating in the smuggling of some blameless electronic equipment. It was held that it was proper to put to the accused the conviction for smuggling heroin of X, who was A's brother and business partner. It was not necessary to give notice of the conviction to the accused prior to the cross-examination. One question which presents itself is whether the conviction would have been admissible if it had been the accused's own rather than his brother's.

7.—Character of Witnesses

13–63 Note 7. Add: *R.* v. *Paraskeva* (1982) 76 Cr.App.R. 162 (C.A.), where a man of previously good character had his conviction quashed because he was not told that the only witness for the prosecution (the victim of an alleged assault) had a *spent* conviction for theft in 1975.

Add: *R.* v. *Smallman* [1982] Crim.L.R. 175 (C.A.). The accused called members of his family as alibi witnesses when he was charged with an indecent assault, whereupon the prosecution cross-examined one of them about a spent conviction of his own (the witness's) for indecent assault. This was held to be a breach of the Practice Direction, because the judge's leave had not first been sought, but it was held also that that was not a ground for upsetting the subsequent conviction. Unless the Practice Direction is of no weight, the decision is best explained as depending on the trial judge's careful direction to the jury to ignore prejudicial matters.

Note 59: Add: See also *R.* v. *McKenney and Pinfold* (1983) 76 Cr.App.R. 271 (C.A.). See below 27–10, 27–32.

CHAPTER 14.—FACTS EXCLUDED BY PUBLIC POLICY

2.—Information for the Detection of Crime

Scope of rule

14–10 The police and prosecuting authorities are protected by public policy from revealing not only the tapes of any telephone intercepts, but whether or not such telephone intercepts have been made: *R.* v. *Guildhall Justices, ex p. the D.P.P.* (1978) 78 Cr.App.R. 269 (D.C.). The reason for the latter half of the rule is that if the answer were in the negative, it might reveal the fact that the police had come by their information by way of an informer. Presumably, as the public interest is involved, there could be no voluntary disclosure either (though it is hard to imagine the apostle of open policing who would make a voluntary disclosure of this sort). See also *R.* v. *Hennessey* (1979) 68 Cr.App.R. 419 (C.A.), where the court upheld a conviction after a similar question had been disallowed by the trial judge. The same public policy was there prayed in aid as justifying the refusal of the prosecuting authorities to disclosure whether or not telephone tapping had been carried out: Lawton L.J. appeared to regard the rule as one capable of being overborne by the circumstances of a particular case, if an accused could see that there was some particular reason why there should be disclosure of the fact or content of telephone intercepts.

NOTE 85. Add *R.* v. *Rankine* [1986] 2 W.L.R. 1075 (C.A.). The rule that the identity of informers may not be disclosed was extended to the identity of the place from which police observations are carried out. The Court based this rule on the need to preserve the utility of the observation post and by the need to protect the occupier of the property from reprisals. The trial judge had discounted the first of these reasons, but the Court of Appeal thought that "the case of the informer is indistinguishable from that of the place of surveillance," and held that even if the police were willing to disclose the identity of the place, the court should intervene. *Quaere* whether these reasons are entirely convincing, and *cf. Webb* v. *Catchlove* (1886) 3 T.L.R. 159 which appears not to have been cited to the court.

R. v. *Hallett* [1986] Crim.L.R. 462 (C.A.). *Held* that the public policy against the disclosure of the identity of informers applies in criminal cases except where the judge decides that the interests of justice require it to be revealed. In such a case, he is bound to permit the evidence to be elicited. This principle is framed in the same sort of language as that which governs the judge's duty in relation to the admissibility of a complainant's sexual history in a prosecution for a sexual offence. In the same way, it is the judge's "duty" to admit the evidence, and no doubt, as in that case, it would be held not to be a discretion (see *R.* v. *Viola, ante*, § 13–53). In this case too one cannot see how the decision when justice requires the evidence to be admitted can sensibly be distinguished from a discretion judicially exercised.

3.—JUDICIAL DISCLOSURES

Private examinations and records in bankruptcy, winding up, lunacy, etc.

14–15 Add at end: There is a large class of cases where statute expressly provides that information of particular classes is not to be disclosed in the course of litigation. Such cases, and their varying approaches to the way in which such protection is to be achieved are discussed in "Public Interest Immunity and Statutory Privilege," Eagles [1983] 42 C.L.J. 118.

4.—THE MODERN SYNTHESIS

14–16 NOTE 23. Add: "Balancing Justice and the Public Interest," Zuckerman (1983) 99 L.Q.R. 14.

14–18 NOTE 50. Add: *ITC Film Distributors* v. *Video Exchange* [1982] 2 All E.R. 241: the public interest in documents being admitted despite the impropriety of the means by which they were obtained is outweighed by the public interest in ensuring that litigants can bring documents into court without fear that they may be stolen by the other party. See also § 15–05 (*infra* and text). *R.* v. *Tompkins* (1977) 67 Cr.App.R. 181 (C.A.), was distinguished on the ground that the public policy question was never raised for consideration in that case. See also *Helliwell* v. *Pigott-Sims* [1980] F.S.R. 356.

NOTE 53. In *Hehir* v. *Commissioner of Police for the Metropolis* [1982] 1 W.L.R. 715 (C.A.), it was held that *Neilson* v. *Laugharne* (see text) led to the result that the statements made in the course of investigations of complaints against the police could not be disclosed so that the makers could be cross-examined on them. In the later case of *Campbell* v. *Tameside* [1982] 3 W.L.R. 74 (C.A.), it was said that the authorities did not compel this conclusion, and *Hehir*'s case (decided by a court of two) was overruled. In the later case, the court ordered discovery of the psychiatric reports on a child alleged to have assaulted a teacher who was suing for negligence, and distinguished a list of authorities of considerable length and weight, including *D.* v. *N.S.P.C.C., Re D, Gaskin* v. *Liverpool City Council* (see text) and *R.* v. *Birmingham Corporation, ex. p. O* [1982] 1 W.L.R. 679 (C.A), where a local authority social services department was held not to be entitled to disclose its files for the purpose of enabling a councillor on the housing committee to investigate the antecedents of proposed foster-parents. In *Peach* v. *Commissioner of Police of the Metropolis* [1986] 2 All E.R. 129 (C.A.), the decision in *Neilson* v. *Laugharne* did not apply to a case where the relevant statements were taken only partly in response to a section 49 complaint, and partly also as part of a general police investigation into a suspicious death. The court ordered discovery of the documents (the Plaintiff being the mother of a young man who died in the course of public disorder and police attempts to quell it). The court might have found the decision easier, had it been aware, as apparently it was not, that *Hehir's* case had been overruled. See also *Cornery* v. *Jacklin* [1985] Crim.L.R. 234 (C.A.) for the case of the policeman who was held entitled to see the complaint made against him. Contrary to the belief expressed in the text, *Lonrho Ltd.* v. *Shell Petroleum* has been reported on the relevant point: see [1980] 1 W.L.R. 627 (H.L.). And see *Continental Reinsurance Corporation* v. *Pine Top Insurance* [1986] 1 Lloyd's Rep. 8 (C.A.) (see *infra*).

NOTE 57. Add: the candour argument waxes and wains. It was expressly relied on the *Birmingham Corporation* case (see last note); but in *Campbell* v. *Tameside* (see last note) both Ackner and O'Connor L.JJ. held that the argument was no longer of any significance. This is a welcome approach, whether or not it was correctly based (as claimed by the Court) on the decision in *S.R.C.* v. *Nasse* [1980] A.C. 1028 (H.L.), which appears to be a case of rather a special kind: see text §§ 15–49, 15–50. In *Air Canada* v. *Secretary of State for Trade (No. 2)* [1983] 2 A.C. 394 (H.L.), the main point decided (see below) was that the applicant would derive insufficient benefit from the disclosure to him of the document even to justify the court inspecting the document for the purpose of ascertaining its potential importance in the litigation: see below § 14–21. There were, however, incidental observations by Lord Fraser (who gave the main speech which appear to adopt and approve the dicta of Lord Wilberforce in the *Burmah Oil* case cited in the text at note 57, and said that this part of Lord Wilberforce's speech was not in conflict with the majority decision in that case: see p. 915e–g. Lord Edmund-Davies and Lord Templeman expressed their agreement with the reasoning of Lord Fraser. Neither the *Thameside* case nor *Nasse*'s case (*supra*) were cited to the House. It is submitted that the dictum approved was cited for the purpose only of urging caution when dealing with documents coming into existence at a high governmental level, and should not be construed as restoring a discredited argument in favour of secrecy. Certainly, Lord Fraser said that there could be disclosure of, for example, cabinet minutes in a case where an issue in litigation involved serious misconduct by a cabinet minister, so that *Sankey* v. *Whitlam* (1978) 21 A.L.R. 505 and *Nixon* v. *U.S.* (1974) 428 U.S. 683 would have been decided in the same way in England. Such cases as these are the ultimate refutation of the candour argument, because the matters which would be disclosed as a result of an order for discovery are the very last things which would be committed to paper if at the time of the creation of the relevant documents it was appreciated that there was a risk that their contents might come out.

14–19 NOTE 65. The decision in *Williams* v. *Home Office* (see text) was at least mentioned without disapproval in the House of Lords in *Home Office* v. *Harman* (see [1982] 2 W.L.R. 338 at 360b, 366a).

14–21 Add NOTE 72a. In *Hehir* v. *Commissioner of Police* [1982] 1 W.L.R. 715 (C.A.), the dicta of Lord Denning M.R. to the effect that public policy immunity could be waived in the case of matters not affecting such matters as security were disapproved; but they were echoed in *Campbell* v. *Tameside* [1982] 3 W.L.R. 74 (C.A.), where it was again said that there could be a waiver in respect of matters falling within "Lord Reid's lower category." Zuckerman (1983) 99 L.Q.R. 14 criticises this approach as too schematic; but in our view there is much to be said for it. The upper tier of cases where the courts refuse to permit disclosure on the ground of public interest is one where the individual predilections of persons in possession of information of vital national importance should not be decisive of or even relevant to the question of whether the information should emerge into the public eye. On the other hand, the widening of the scope of public interest immunity so that it may be claimed in an appropriate case by officials of many public and semi-public bodies involves the possibility of a very large range of cases where the objection ought to be raised. It seems odd that the Court is bound to look for and take the point *proprio motu*, and that the relevant officials cannot even willingly disclose information necessary for a fair trial, especially as the criteria by which the public interest is judged are now so much wider than at the time the rule against waiver was first formulated, Of course, when it comes to documents relevant to matters such as national security or high level government policy, there is much more to be said for prohibition on the disclosure being absolute. This is particularly true given that it is possible to waive privilege unintentionally, for example by disclosing a document referring expressly to another document which plainly ought not to be disclosed. It is submitted that a dictum in *Air Canada* v. *Secretary of State for Trade (No. 2)* [1983] 2 A.C. 394 (H.L.), at 436A (*per* Lord Fraser) to the effect that public policy immunity cannot be waived by the Crown or by any party is directed at the class of case which was then before the House, namely a case falling unequivocally and admittedly in the upper category. Equally, if this class of case is narrowly circumscribed, as we think it to be, the benefits of the possibility of a waiver of immunity are considerable. It is not merely that isolated officials might accidentally or wittingly take steps which would have the effect of waiving privilege and thus promoting fairness in litigation in individual cases. The very fact that there can be a waiver will immunise a properly cautious official against the fear of inadvertently creating a precedent for disclosure. See also Eagles in [1983] 42 C.L.J. 118, where it is pointed out that in a case where documents are withheld from production on the ground that the information contained in them was supplied by persons who are entitled to have their anonymity protected, it is relevant to know what is the attitude of those persons to the disclosure of the documents in question in the particular case.

NOTE 86. Add: see *Air Canada* v. *Secretary of State for Trade (No. 2)* (*supra*) has added yet another twist to an already tangled skein. In that case, the British Airports Authority had raised their landing charges by some 35 per cent. after the Government had informed them that the new terminals could not be financed by the state, and that the funds for their construction had to be found out of revenue generated by the airports themselves. An action was brought by a number of airlines against the Secretary of State and the Authority on the grounds that the raising of the charges was *ultra vires*, having been decided upon by reference to the Government's policy of reducing the P.S.B.R., which, it was said, was a matter which ought not to have been taken into account. Discovery was given of the documents passing between the Secretary of State and the Authority which related to the increase, but what was not disclosed were the interministerial communications and the preparatory documents used by the relevant Ministers at the meetings where the proposed increases were discussed. At first instance ([1983] 1 All E.R. 161), Bingham J. held, notwithstanding the Secretary of State certifying the public interest required that the documents be withheld, that they should be produced for his inspection. He observed (at pp. 165–6) that "one need not be a radical advocate of government in the sunshine to feel that the protection afforded to official documents in the past has perhaps been somewhat overgenerous." With this dictum we respectfully agree, but both the Court of Appeal (*ibid.*) the House of Lords (*supra*) held that the documents ought not to be produced even for the inspection of the judge alone. The decision is in effect a development of the reasoning in the *Burmah Oil* case (see text), because all the speeches in the House of Lords were primarily concerned with the criteria by reference to which an application for discovery could be justified; and this question was distinct from (but held to be connected with) the one which would arise at a later stage in the inquiry, namely whether the public interest demanded that the documents should be withheld even if they *were* clearly "necessary . . . for fairly disposing of the cause or matter": see *per* Lord Edmund-Davies at p. 1125B. The leading opinion was that of Lord Fraser, and he distinguished between the "relevance" which would require a document to be disclosed in ordinary litigation, and that which was required where a plea of public interest immunity was raised. In the latter case, disclosure is required only when the trial judge forms the view that the disputed document will significantly assist the party seeking discovery. This is so both at the stage where the judge has to consider whether or not a document ought to be inspected by him, and, if such inspection be ordered, when consideration comes to be given to whether or not the other party ought to be allowed to see it. Lord Wilberforce and Edmund-Davies followed broadly the same line. Lord Templeman and Lord Scarman agreed with the result reached by the rest of the House, but took the view that the documents ought to be inspected if they would materially advance the case of *either* party. The House was therefore agreed in rejecting the criterion of relevance in favour of a test of substantial benefit in the litigation resulting from disclosure. There are, with respect, serious objections to the approach the courts must now adopt. First, one reason for the difference in the application of the rules about discovery in this class of case is said to lie in the fact that the judge will not have the assistance of counsel if he merely looks at the documents by himself in order to ascertain whether or not they should be disclosed. It is not clear why this will lead to any danger other than those which flow from the fact that a judge will, in the nature of things, be less able to perceive the potential assistance to a party's case than the latter's legal representatives. This means that there would be no question of disclosure of such documents except in a clear case. It is important to observe that the inspection which was under consideration was *not* for the purpose of deciding whether the public interest was in favour of disclosure or not, but merely for the purpose of ascertaining whether or not the documents were relevant. Secondly, it is obscure how a judge can divine in every case the contents of material contained in documents he has not seen and the likely consequences for the litigation if they are disclosed. Indeed in the *Air Canada* case itself, Bingham J. at first instance found himself unable to decide whether or not the disclosure documents would assist the applicants, and that there were indications both ways. The reason he thought that the documents ought to be inspected by him was that "it would be wrong to guess." This, with respect, is precisely the exercise which the decision of the House of Lords requires. The exercise conducted by Lord Wilberforce (*ibid.* at pp. 920e–921a) is an illustration of the way in which speculation of a rather abstract sort will have to be prayed in aid of substitution for the judge inspecting the documents and forming his own view. While the *Air Canada* case itself may be a case where it was possible to be sure that the documents could not possibly assist the applicant (though this was not the trial judge's view), that can hardly be something which will be applicable to every conceivable case in the future where such a point is taken. Thirdly, it is hard to see how the result reached in the *Air Canada* case is consistent with the *Burmah Oil* case, where inspection was ordered without any finding of fact by any tribunal that it was more likely than not that what was unearthed would be of assistance to the applicants; and, of course, in that case the documents, once inspected by the House of Lords, were found to be of such trifling significance that they should not be disclosed to the party seeking discovery. Fourthly, one justification for the criterion of relevance which obtains in ordinary proceedings is that it is often not possible to tell at an early stage in litigation what will and what will not assist one's case. The task of the trial judge, informed only of the issues between the parties, would be still more difficult. It may not be particularly easy to satisfy a court as to the relevance of a document when no more can be done than point to the issues between the parties, but it is at least an intelligible mental process which the judge is being asked to undertake. To assess the potential *benefit* to a party of disclosure of a document whose content is unknown is not a task which a judge could embark on with confidence. Fifthly, if the criterion is not relevance but the likelihood that the applicant will be assisted by the disclosure of admittedly relevant material, the interlocutory process is likely to be contaminated by an investigation of the merits of the whole case, on the facts and the law. It must be relevant to the question of the utility of disclosure to know whether or not the applicant's case is likely to succeed if he can only prove the right facts. This will mean that the trial judge will be expected either to take a preliminary and (necessarily) superficial view of the case, which is hardly desirable, or that he will be invited to deal with the whole case in detail at an interlocutory stage, which would truly be an absurdity.

All these actual and potential disadvantages of the ruling might be justified if the public interest was necessarily served thereby. But the process described above takes place merely because a claim to public interest immunity has been made, not because it has been made out. Nor is the risk against which the decision is said to guard that there should be disclosure to the world at large, or even to the parties, of highly confidential documents. It is the private inspection of the documents by the trial judge which is prevented. It is respectfully submitted that the decision goes too far in its protection of the executive, and should, at the least, be confined to documents which come into existence at the very highest reaches of the state.

In *Continental Reinsurance Corporation* v. *Pine Top Insurance Ltd.* [1986] 1 Lloyd's Rep. 8 (C.A.), the Plaintiffs' claim against reinsurers was met by a plea of non-disclosure and similar defences, based on the way in which the Plaintiffs had underwritten business. The Plaintiffs had been in contact with the Department of Trade because the directors were concerned at the way in which the company had been run and whether there was a sufficient margin of solvency, so that the help of the Department could be obtained in setting things right. The defendants sought discovery of these communications. The Department sought to prevent their production on the footing that they fell into a class of documents disclosure of which would be injurious to the public interest, and to have set aside a subpoena ad testificandum which had been served on the official involved in the relevant exchange of correspondence. It was *held* that the documents in question were not of the kind to which immunity attaches almost automatically because they reveal the inner workings of government at the highest level (as in the *Burmah Oil* case (see text), nor "low level" documents where the claim for immunity seems weak. They were rather of a class for which confidentiality is claimed on the ground that it is necessary to maintain the flow of information to the executive. Secondly, in the case of documents in this category, even where it was established that there is a valid argument for confidentiality on this ground, the court is nonetheless entitled to look at the documents and balance the public interest in favour of preserving the executive's sources of information against that in favour of disclosure. It was said that in the case of "low level" documents, the court will inspect before ordering disclosure in order to check that the claim for immunity in order to check that the claim for immunity is ill-founded. (This seems a different approach from that which appears in the earlier authorities.) Thirdly, although the information in question could have been required by the Department to be disclosed, and the statutory provisions which conferred these powers on the department provide for a correlative protection from disclosure, that does not amount to a reason for the withholding of discovery in a case where the information is in fact voluntarily disclosed.

It was held that the judge was justified in inspecting the documents, though (a) he should first have given separate consideration to the question of how likely that would be to reveal grounds for overriding public interest immunity; but that (b) the *Air Canada* case (*supra*) shows that inspection should not be undertaken as a routine operation. But once the documents were inspected, a balancing exercise had to be carried out. The balance is (*semble*) weighted in favour of immunity, and the material disclosed did not alter that position. The subpoena was not set aside, because there were other matters about which the departmental representative could give evidence; but he could not be asked about the matters to which the immunity attached.

CHAPTER 15.—FACTS EXCLUDED BY PRIVILEGE

Effect when allowed

15–05 NOTE 18. But see *ITC Film Distributors* v. *Video Exchange* [1982] 2 All E.R. 241: see above § 14–18. See also *Goddard* v. *Nationwide Building Society* [1986] 3 W.L.R. 734 (C.A.) which appears to create an important exception to the principle of *Calcraft* v. *Guest* (see text).

1.—PROFESSIONAL CONFIDENCES

15–09 NOTE 60a. *A.-G.* v. *Lundin* [1982] Crim.L.R. 296 (D.C.).

Scope of employment

15–12 NOTE 74. Add *Re Sarah C Getty Trust* [1985] 2 All E.R. 809.

Criminal proceedings

15–13 NOTES 88–9. Add *R.* v. *King* (1983) 77 Cr.App.R. 1 (C.A.). The decision in *Truman (Frank) Export Ltd.* v. *M.P.C.* (see text) has been repudiated, and the decision in *R.* v. *Peterborough Justices* (see text) preferred. Although communications between a solicitor and an expert witness are privileged, the mere fact that documents or things are sent by the solicitor to the expert for his opinion does not render them privileged from production, nor is his report of itself privileged unless it attracts the privilege for some other reason.

Communications in furtherance of an illegal object

15–14 NOTE 92. Add *Banque Keyser Ullmann S.A.* v. *Skandia (U.K.) Insurance Co. Ltd.* [1986] 1 Lloyd's Rep. 536. The rationale of the rule in *R.* v. *Cox and Railton* is not that it assists the court in determining whether or not a fraud has been committed but that communications to a solicitor in furtherance of a crime or fraud do not take place in the course of a professional legal relationship. Thus a bank which had taken an assignment of certain insurance policies and which subsequently brought an action on those policies was entitled to legal professional privilege in relation to communications passing between them and their legal advisers, whether for legal advice or in contemplation of litigation, notwithstanding that the assignor was alleged to have obtained the insurance on the strength of a fraudulent valuation.

Communications with third parties

15–18 NOTE 31. Add: *re Highgrade Traders The Times*, 20th December, 1983; *McAvan* v. *L.T.E.* (1983) 133 N.L.J. 1101 (C.A.).

NOTE 34. Add *The Aegis Blaze* [1986] 1 Lloyd's Rep. 203 (C.A.). See *infra* § 15–19 n. 44.

NOTES 34–36. See also *Re Sarah C Getty Trust* [1985] 2 All E.R. 809.

In *Lee* v. *South West Thames R.H.A.* [1985] 2 All E.R. 385 (C.A.), the Plaintiff suffered brain damage either in hospital or in the course of an ambulance journey between two hospitals. The hospitals were run by Regional Health Authorities A and B, and the ambulance service by Authority C. Discovery was sought from all three Authorities pursuant to section 33(2)(b) of the Supreme Court Act 1981 (which enables discovery to be obtained from potential parties in advance of the commencement of proceedings). C (the ambulance Authority) claimed privilege for a copy of a report prepared by them and sent to A at the latter's request. The latter had asked for the report because they wished to put it before their solicitors. At the time they did so, no proceedings were contemplated against C. It was held that the document was privileged in the hands of C, even though the privilege was entirely that of A.

The Court of Appeal expressed themselves to be dissatisfied with this result (see *ibid.* at 389h), because it left the Plaintiff with no means of establishing the cause of his injury. It is not clear to us as a matter of policy that the person who voluntarily makes documentary material available to a party or potential party to litigation should thereby expose himself to the risk of having to produce that document to his own detriment. No doubt hardship would be caused in individual cases; but that is potentially true of every case in which privilege is claimed. If the Plaintiff in this case had been able to mount an action against C on the basis of the memorandum, it would have been entirely fortuitous, and would have infringed all those policies which the law of privilege advances.

That said, the bounds of privilege are drawn in a technical way, and it by no means follows that the law gives general effect to the policy of encouraging parties to litigation to obtain information, evidence and advice without fear of the consequences to the extent of protecting the sources as well as the recipients. The Court of Appeal recognised that in holding that the privilege is that of A alone and not C's privilege at all, so that A could at any time waive the privilege (see at p. 389e). Accordingly, the question of whether C is or is not required to produce the document must be a matter of chance whichever rule is applied, given that C is not to be given an independent privilege of his own. There is a good deal to be said for leaving people in C's position to take their own decisions as to whether or not to give information when they are not compelled to do so. They will be protected by the defamation species of privilege from actions for slander or libel; and if they choose to expose themselves to the risks of litigation arising out of the very incident upon which their testimony is given, there can only be a chance benefit for an otherwise disadvantaged Plaintiff. (In cases where they are not sued, no doubt their possession of a copy of the document is only as agent for the party for whom the document was produced, and so would not be produced on subpoena.)

There is a powerful argument to the effect that if C is compelled to disclose the document to the Plaintiff, the Plaintiff has found a way inside A's privilege. This consideration is one which the Court took seriously in *Lee*'s case (although they adverted to it only briefly), and it may indeed have been the foundation of the decision; see at 389f. The dilemma is no new one, however, and in the past has always been resolved in favour of the destruction of the privilege. The doctrine of *Calcraft* v. *Guest* (see text) whereby copies of privileged documents are not themselves protected by privilege is directly in point, although not adverted to by the Court of Appeal.

Nor was the question free from authority. In *Schneider* v. *Leigh* [1955] 2 Q.B. 195 (C.A.) (a decision binding on the Court of Appeal), a medical expert had made a report to the solicitors for the defendants in a personal injuries action. The latter had disclosed part of that report, whereupon the plaintiff in that action had sued the expert for defamation. It was held that no legal professional privilege attached to the copy of the report which the expert had retained, because the privilege was that of the defendant in the personal injuries action. This decision was distinguished in *Lee*'s case on the ground that the cause of action against C was not a wholly independent cause of action, but arose out of the same incident. With respect, we can see that the difference exists, but are unable to perceive in it any justification for different treatment of the two cases; nor can we see how the decision in *Calcraft* v. *Guest* can be evaded. (There may be more doubt about this proportion since the decision in *Goddard* v. *Nationwide Building Society* [1986] 3 W.L.R. 734 (C.A.), reported too late for detailed consideration in this Supplement.)

The decision in *Buttes Gas and Oil Co.* v. *Hammer* [1981] Q.B. 223 (C.A.) was also distinguished on the footing that while there may be such a thing as "common interest" privilege, there was no common interest here between A and C. Each party might well end up trying to lay the liability at the door of the other.

In the result, then, the Court of Appeal found themselves compelled to refuse disclosure, although there were reasons of policy why they wished to take the opposite line. As appears from the above, we think that those particular policy reasons are not very powerful; that there are other, stronger, policy reasons which might justify disclosure; but that these have been taken into account in all the traditional analyses of legal professional privilege and have been held to be outweighed by other factors affecting the general policy of that privilege. It is also submitted with respect that a contrary conclusion was required by binding authority.

Duration of privilege

15–19 NOTE 44. Add: but see now *the Aegis Blaze* [1986] 1 Lloyd's Rep. 203 (C.A.) where a survey report obtained by a P. & I. Club for the purposes of defending a suit for cargo damage against a shipowner whose vessel was entered with the Club was held privileged as against a different cargo-owner suing the same shipowner in respect of different damage to different cargo sustained on a different voyage. The principle "once privileged, always privileged" accordingly applies even though (a) the subject-matter of the dispute is different, (b) the parties to the dispute are different, and (c) the communication was not between solicitor and client but between solicitor and third party in contemplation of litigation. Insofar as *Kerry Council* v. *Liverpool Association* (see text) decided anything to the contrary (the Court of Appeal in *the Aegis Blaze* in fact held that it stood for no particular principle), it does not represent the law.

Waiver

15–20 One of the most difficult problems of the law relating to waiver of privilege is the extent to which documents mentioned in or connected with a document in respect of which privilege has been waived become liable themselves to disclosure. This has recently been addressed by the decision of Hobhouse J. in *General Accident Fire and Life Assurance Corp. Ltd.* v. *Tanter* [1984] 1 W.L.R. 100, where two distinctions were identified, namely (a) between documents which had been merely disclosed and documents which were actually tendered in evidence; and (b) between the specified transaction the subject of a document in respect of which privilege is waived and the content of that transaction. In an action brought by an insurance company against reinsurance underwriters and certain brokers, there was a cross-claim by the underwriters against some of the brokers. A Civil Evidence Act Notice was served by those brokers in respect of a note of a conversation in which certain matters were said to have been discussed between representatives of the brokers and the underwriters. The note was itself privileged having been prepared for the brokers' solicitors. Prior to the maker of the note being called to give evidence, the note was put to the relevant underwriter in cross-examination, and he continued to deny the terms of the note. It was contended that by putting the document to the witness, privilege had been waived over the note and all documents relating to matters mentioned in the note, including, for example, the instructions to counsel and proofs of evidence so far as relevant to the matters discussed in the conversation referred to in the note. It was held that privilege in the note itself was waived by the service of the notice, but that the application was premature because the note did not become evidence merely by being put to a witness in cross-examination (as the procedure followed was characterised). It would not do so until it was introduced in evidence, either to refresh the maker's memory or, by leave of the court under the Civil Evidence Act 1968. Hobhouse J. went on to hold that there was no waiver of privilege over any other documents unless and until the document was tendered in evidence. He distinguished *Burnell* v. *B.T.C.* [1956] 1 Q.B. 187, *Great Atlantic Insurance Co.* v. *Home Insurance Co.* (see text, n. 54) and *The Athanasia Comninos* (text, n. 51) on the ground that in those cases the documents in question were actually "deployed in evidence." While that is so as a matter of fact, it does not appear that it was relied on by the judges in these cases as a ground of decision. Hobhouse J. also held that *Doland (George) Ltd.* v. *Blackburn & Co. Ltd.* (text, n. 58) was either to be confined to its own facts or was wrongly decided. Certainly, there are difficulties with a waiver whose extent turns on the distinction between privilege attaching to professional confidences and that which is attracted by communications passing between solicitors and third parties in contemplation of litigation.

It is, however, respectfully submitted that there are difficulties also with the part of the judgment of Hobhouse J. which holds that the test for a waiver of associated documents is whether or not the source document has itself been proffered in evidence. This conclusion may have been induced by the way in which the argument proceeded before him. Hobhouse J. rightly identified a waiver as having taken place in relation to the note of the conversation when the Civil Evidence Act Notice was served. Insofar as the waiver of privilege extended beyond the note itself, it is hard to see how it could make any difference whether or not the document was formally tendered in evidence. The judge was much influenced by considerations of fairness; but that commodity is not a desideratum only in the course of actions which proceed to trial. Settlements take place on the basis of the discovery between the parties, and it can hardly be right that a party can selectively waive privilege at the time of serving his list of documents, on the basis that the loss of privilege is confined to the documents disclosed unless there is a trial *and* the documents are put in evidence. It was held indeed that it was only if they were put in evidence *by the party who originally disclosed it* that any question of the extent of the waiver arose at all. It is true that the effect of a waiver might be very extensive; but it is submitted that this might equally be so whether the doctrine came to apply before the hearing or only in the light of evidence put forward during the course of it. Moreover, as mentioned below, the judgment in the instant case itself goes far to mitigate the most extreme and unfortunate consequences of what might be termed the doctrine of associative waiver. It is respectfully submitted that, in the case under consideration, on service of the statutory Notice the waiver was complete, and the underwriters were entitled at that stage to any further discovery to which that waiver had exposed the brokers.

Hobhouse J. went on to consider the extent of the waiver. He identified the major problem which arises from the doctrine that a waiver of privilege over one document carries with it the waiver of privilege over associated documents, which is that it can lead to an infinite regress as more and more privileged documents are compelled to be disclosed because their contents have a subject-matter common to another document already disclosed. The solution reached by the learned judge was to confine the waiver to documents relating to the transaction described by the relevant document, rather than all the matters to which the transaction was relevant. In the instant case, it was held that even if the document became evidence, privilege would be waived only in respect of what was said by the maker of the document at the relevant meeting, and would not extend to what he said to later dates in conversation with his solicitors. It is thought, with respect, that even on the restrictive view of the extent of the waiver, it must go further than merely to the words used by the maker of the document. It should surely extend to all connected documents relating to the fact of the conversation having taken place, the personnel present, the terms of the discussion, etc. That, however, would not require disclosure of all documents relating to matters discussed in the course of that conversation. It is respectfully submitted that the learned judge was right in holding that the link between the document disclosed and those it carries with it in its train has to be more than a mere common subject-matter.

It may be that a real difficulty lies in ascertaining what is a "connected" document. This is something which has not been very deeply considered by the authorities, and the position is therefore somewhat confused at present; it is thought that the distinction drawn by Hobhouse J. between transaction and subject-matter is potentially a fruitful one, even though we respectfully disagree with the way in which it was said to be applicable in the instant case.

NOTE 56. Add: and where a list of documents had been served and inspection had taken place, there was a waiver of privilege in relation to all documents enumerated in it including some for which privilege had by mistake not been claimed. Notes had been taken and at least one photocopy made, so that secondary evidence of the documents could be given; but the party to whom discovery had been inadvertently given was entitled to put the best evidence, that is the documents themselves, before the court. It would have been otherwise if the mistake had been detected before inspection had taken place: *re Briamore Manufacturing Ltd.* [1986] 3 All E.R. 132.

3.—MATRIMONIAL COMMUNICATIONS

15–34 Add at end: there are certain statutory exceptions to the privilege against self-crimination which extend to questions to the spouse of the accused. See text § 15–45 and below.

4.—CRIMINATING QUESTIONS

Scope of the rule

15–38 Add at end: NOTE 46a. In *R.* v. *Nottingham JJ ex p. Lynn* (1984) 79 Cr.App.R. 238 (D.C.), *Williams* v. *Summerfield* (see text) was followed and the decisions in *Waterhouse* v. *Barker* (see text) and *South Staffs Tram Co.* v. *Ebsmith* [1895] 2 Q.B. 669 were held to be of authority only for civil proceedings.

Oath of witness necessary but not conclusive

15–39 NOTE 50. Add: in *Khan* v. *Khan* [1982] 2 All E.R. 60 (C.A.), it was held that it is not merely where there is a minimal risk of prosecution that the privilege is negatived: where there is already a substantial risk that the witness will be prosecuted in respect of the matters about which he declines to answer questions, it is necessary to show that answering will increase that risk before the privilege can be invoked.

Exceptions to the rule

15–45 NOTE 85. Add: *Khan* v. *Khan* (above), where it was held that the removal of the protection of the privilege against self-crimination by section 31(1) of the Theft Act 1968 was not affected by the fact that the same facts as gave rise to a charge under that Act might also be the subject of a prosecution for some other offence to which the privilege *prima facie* attached.

15–45 NOTE 87. Add: the limitation on the privilege against self-crimination established by the Supreme Court Act 1981, section 72(1), is not to be construed restrictively—see *Universal City Studios Inc.* v. *Hubbard* [1984] 1 All E.R. 661 (C.A.) 2 W.L.R. 882.

6.—PROTECTION INDEPENDENT OF PRIVILEGE

(a) *No use of evidence for other purposes*

15–48 NOTE 98. The principle in *Riddick* v. *Thames Board Mills* (see text) has certain limitations. In *Sony Corporation* v. *Time Electronics* [1981] 1 W.L.R. 1293, an injunction had been obtained by the Plaintiffs to enable them to prevent dishonest trading on the part of the Defendants. On visiting the Defendants' premises to serve the injunction, the Plaintiffs' representatives discovered other counterfeit goods of the kind manufactured by the Plaintiffs, but not the subject of the original order. A test purchase verified the fact that the goods were counterfeit; and it was held that a new action could be brought against the Defendants in respect of the fresh infringement. It was said to be founded on the test purchase and not on the original Order, and thus not to fall within the *Ridd ick* principle.

15–48 NOTES 7–8. In *Home Office* v. *Harman* [1982] 2 W.L.R. 338 (H.L.), the decision of the Court of Appeal was upheld (see text). It was in effect held that although it might have been the case that all the documents disclosed by the appellant solicitor to a journalist would have been available to the latter if he had obtained a copy of the official transcript of the tape-recording of the proceedings, it did not follow that one who was charged with the responsibility for using the documents only for the purposes of her client could put them to some other use altogether. It was recognised that this might put litigants and their legal advisers in a less favourable position as regards disclosure of documents used at a hearing than ordinary members of the public, but the majority regarded this as a theoretical and not a practical objection. Moreover, "the implied obligation not to make improper use of discovered documents is . . . independent of any obligation under the general law relating to confidentiality" (*per* Lord Keith at p. 349F). The apparent anomaly of the contemptuous breach of confidence being committed in respect of a document which had been made public pursuant to a constitutional principle that it be so appeared overwhelming to Lords Simon and Scarman who dissented, and indeed went so far as to opine that even documents which had not actually been read out in court, but which had been made exhibits at the trial could be disclosed without a contempt being committed, because they had entered the public domain. Even the dissentients recognised that either result led to anomalies, and it is respectfully submitted that the majority were right to distinguish between the purpose of public oral hearings and the incidental consequences which might follow from them. As noted in the text (§§ 14–19 and 20), a contrary decision might lead to a still more restrictive view being taken of the documents which the public interest permits to be disclosed. See *Disclosure of Material Obtained on Discovery*, I. Eagles (1984) 47 M.L.R. 284 for vehement, but in our view unconvincing, criticism. See *Sybron Corporation* v. *Barclays Bank*, *The Times*, March 9, 1984.

(c) *Discretionary control over procedure generally*

15–51 NOTE 38. Add *Format* v. *I.T.T.* [1983] F.S.R. 473.
NOTE 39. Add: *Campbell* v. *Tameside* [1982] 3 W.L.R. 74 (C.A.).

CHAPTER 16.—THE RULE AGAINST HEARSAY

16–05 NOTE 28. Add: *R.* v. *Blastland* [1986] A.C. 41 (H.L.), B was charged with the murder of a small boy. He sought to call witnesses to certify that prior to the discovery of the body, another man, M, had told them that a boy had been murdered. It was held by the Court of Appeal that this evidence was rightly excluded as hearsay; but the House of Lords upheld the decision to exclude the testimony rather on the ground that it was insufficiently relevant and probative. It is established that statements illustrative of a relevant state of mind are not hearsay: *Lloyd* v. *Powell Duffrys Steam Coal Co.* [1914] A.C. 733. The purpose for which the accused wished to rely on M's statement was to show that he was as likely as B to have committed the murder. As a statement by M directly admitting the murder would have been inadmissible, the House of Lords held that the proof of a statement falling short of an admission as circumstantial evidence of guilt was even more objectionable. The fact that he had knowledge of the fact of the murder was consistent with any number of explanations and was therefore not of itself probative of guilt. (Similar reasoning was applied to the false alibi given by a person other than the accused when questioned by the police in *R.* v. *Steel* (1981) 73 Cr.App.R. 173 (C.A.).)

There are powerful arguments in favour of this result, especially given that every notorious murder apparently attracts a crop of false confessions. Nonetheless, the reasoning of the House of Lords in *R.* v. *Blastland* is, with respect, not altogether convincing. The fact that a direct admission would be inadmissible *as an admission* does not entail that it could in no circumstances be admitted as evidence that the *de cujus* had knowledge consistent only with his presence at a specific occasion. Again, where a man is charged with murder by stabbing, it must surely be relevant to show that a third party was at the scene of the crime, and that a short time later he was found covered with blood, or with a newly cleaned knife in his possession. No doubt at any given moment many people have blood on their clothes from domestic accidents or for any number of reasons; and the knife might be equally explicable in several ways. That goes to the weight of the evidence; but it does not demonstrate that it should be ruled out altogether. In *R.* v. *Blastland*, the accused admitted to having been with the boy shortly before his murder, and claimed to have seen a man whom he described. M's appearance in fact corresponded with that description, and he had made, and subsequently retracted, a number of admissions to the police. No-one sought to introduce the admissions (which in the particular case added nothing admissible to the statements which the defence sought to introduce). The case was a strong one against B on the facts; and what is legally relevant must be a question of degree. The case is perhaps an illustration of the limitations of both jury trial and adversarial procedure. In an objective inquiry without the constraints, real or supposed, of jurors' inexperience, those conducting the case would surely have called M to give an account of himself and to enable the accused's representatives to cross-examine him. There are no doubt risks that jurors will be confused by bogus confessions; but a confession by a man who revealed knowledge of the murder before the public came to know of it is difficult to ignore. If the case against B was a strong one, M's knowledge and even his confession might be rejected by the jury: and if it was not a strong one, or if it was no stronger than the case against B, a jury might be thought entitled to entertain a reasonable doubt. At all events, we think with respect that the reasoning on which the evidence was held to be irrelevant is fallacious, and that if it was to be excluded on that ground, the justifications are different. It is perhaps significant that both the trial judge and the Court of Appeal excluded the evidence not for that reason, but because they thought that it was hearsay. This was not the basis of the decision in the House of Lords and it is implicit in the opinions of their Lordships that it was not.

16–08 NOTE 35. Add: *the Scope of the Hearsay Rule*, Stephen Guest (1985) 101 L.Q.R. 385.

1.—THE RULE AT COMMON LAW

16–10 NOTE 63. The difficulties latent in this area surfaced in formation in *R.* v. *O'Brien* [1982] Crim.L.R. 746 and *R.* v. *Okorodu* [1982] Crim.L.R. 747, in which cases in the Crown Court one judge permitted photofit evidence to be put before the jury, and the other did not. It is not clear from the reports that the possible hearsay objection lay at the bottom of the refusal to admit the evidence.

In *R.* v. *Kelsey* (1982) 74 Cr.App.R. 213 (C.A.), it was held that A may refresh his memory from a document written by B, even though he was merely told of the contents of the document by B and did not see it himself. With respect, this decision appears to permit a clear infringement of the hearsay rule. See also *Re Attorney-General's Reference (No. 3 of 1979)* (1979) 69 Cr.App.R. 411 (C.A.).

Documents

NOTE 68. Add: until it is proved that the witness is the maker of or party to a document, it should not be before the jury—see *R.* v. *Cooper* (1986) 82 Cr.App.R. 74 (C.A.).

16–11 NOTE 73. Add: *R.* v. *Pettigrew* (1980) 71 Cr.App.R. 39 (C.A.) (see text § 18–03), has been criticised on the ground that it was unnecessary to invoke the Criminal Evidence Act 1965 in that case, because the evidence of the computer selection was original evidence and not hearsay (see, *e.g.* [1980] Crim.L.R. 239). In *R.* v. *Wood* (1982) 76 Cr.App.R. 23 (C.A.), data obtained from computer analyses of the chemical composition of certain metals which were subsequently stolen were subsequently compared with the results of an analysis of metals found in the accused's possession. *R.* v. *Pettigrew* was distinguished on the ground that the evidence in question was admissible without resort to the Act, because there was no hearsay involved. (For commentary supporting the decision, see [1982] Crim.L.R. 667; and *cf. R.* v. *Wiles* [1982] Crim.L.R. 669 for further commentary.) It is thought that there is a real hearsay difficulty in the way of the admission of evidence such as this. It is of course right to say that the mere fact that the results could have been obtained laboriously by individuals rather than swiftly by computer is not relevant to the question of whether or not the evidence was hearsay. But the reason that the evidence was admissible in *R.* v. *Wood* was that the prosecution were able to call the individual who had programmed the computer, and those who had run the program he had prepared. The printouts were in effect a joint statement by all those persons. But this result will not be possible in all cases. The results produced by the computer are not thought out by the computer. They are a statement by those who programmed the computer so that the product of certain data, may be provided by the computer by mechanical means where a human would have had to employ deductive reasoning. If those who programmed the computer failed to take account of one combination of individual items of data, the computer would produce a wrong answer. This would not be because the computer had made a mistake, but because the programmer had made an inaccurate statement as to the result of a particular constellation of data. In other words, the computer printouts were no more than a statement by the programmers and the users of the computer; that is, it would have been hearsay, had those individuals not been called. It is true that the court drew the analogy of a mechanical device for recording data, but such cases may themselves be suspect, and in any event did not resemble the instant case, where it appears that all the relevant programmers as well as users gave evidence. (In practice, this may oversimplify the position, because it is likely in most cases that there will be a hierarchy of programs run on the computer, of which the program run by the analysts would represent only the top tier.)

No doubt it is an absurd and inconvenient result, given the inherent reliability of information supplied by computers, that the programmer and users should have to be called in every case, especially as there are likely to be cases of commercially available programs where the former at least are unavailable, or even unknown. However, it is the fact that the computer, when operating correctly, is incapable of making a mistake, whereas its programmers are not, that makes the results hearsay.

A further example of the confusion of thought which pervades the subject of evidence derived from computer is to be found in *R.* v. *Ewing* [1983] Q.B. 1039 (C.A.), where it appears to have been assumed that it was the personal knowledge of the *operator* alone which was relevant. See also *R.* v. *Nicholls* (1976) 63 Cr.App.R. 187 (C.A.); *R.* v. *Van Vreden* (1973) 57 Cr.App.R. 818 (C.A.).

On the other hand mechanical devices do not always function correctly. Yet in *Hughes* v. *McConnell* [1986] 1 All E.R. 268 (D.C.) it was held that circumstantial evidence which, if accepted, would invalidate the finding of a Lion Intoximeter as to the amount of alcohol present in a breath sample is inadmissible. Only evidence going directly to the reliability of the machine was held admissible.

It would be better if the common law rule against hearsay were reformulated so as to avoid the problem arising. A broader view of what constitute trade records for the purposes of the Criminal Evidence Act 1965 would also solve the problem in most cases. In the case of banking records, the Bankers' Books Evidence Act 1879, as amended by Sched. 6 to the Banking Act 1979, will also often provide a solution to the problem of admissibility posed by computer records.

Note 76. Add: *Reliability, Hearsay and the English Criminal Trial*, Ashworth and Pattenden (1986) 102 L.Q.R. 292.

Extrinsic sources of knowledge

16–13 Add at end: In *R.* v. *Shone* (1983) 76 Cr.App.R. 72 (C.A.), it was held that evidence could be given of the absence of an entry on a stock record card to support the prosecution's case that certain vehicle springs had been stolen. Had the springs been sold or used in a repair, there should have been an entry on the card. *R.* v. *Patel* [1981] 3 All E.R. 94 (C.A.), was distinguished on the ground that those responsible for the compilation and maintenance of the records were not called to give evidence, whereas in the instant case they were. The contention that the evidence of the records was hearsay was rejected, on the ground that the absence of an entry relating to the springs was circumstantial evidence that they had neither been sold nor used. It is not clear that the decision can stand with *Myers* v. *D.P.P.* (see text), because the source of the information in the records was not said to be the personal knowledge of the compiler. If there had been an entry rather than the absence of an entry in the records relied on by the prosecution, it would not assist that the person who made that entry was called, if that person was not the ultimate source of the information leading to the entry. The absence of a mark in the records amounted to the absence of an assertion by any one of the persons responsible for the distribution of springs that they had been sold or used in repair, and the personal knowledge of the compiler of the record cards did not go beyond that. It may seem that this is a rather theoretical objection to the admissibility of the evidence in *R.* v. *Shone*, but the rule against hearsay, in its present form, is a very technical one. It is possible in many cases to reach a sensible result by reference to the statutory exceptions, but it is thought that the requirements of legislation and construction are more clearly discernible if the rule is consistently applied. The actual decision in *R.* v. *Shone* could be supported on the basis that the report does not say that anyone other than the compiler of the records was responsible for the supply of the information on which they were based, even if that seems rather unlikely. As indicated above, however, that is not what the Court actually decided, which was that an inference could be drawn from the absence of information in the records themselves. That amounts to holding that the system was itself a source of circumstantial evidence and did not involve a statement by anyone: see also *R.* v. *Abadom* (1983) 76 Cr.App.R. 48 at 52 (C.A.). It is with respect submitted that this approach has the effect of resurrecting the notion of a document which "speaks its face" (even if only by the blankness of its countenance), discredited in *Myers* v. *D.P.P.* If one supposes a case on facts similar to those in *R.* v. *Shone*, except that a daily tick in the records indicated that the springs had not been sold or used, it would at once be apparent that what was relied on was not the system itself but the truth of the entry in the records. In effect, the decision would be correct if the word in the second sentence of this note read "would" rather than "should."

The position is different where it is the total absence of a document rather than the absence of an entry in an existing document which gives rise to the inference that a particular transaction has or has not taken place: see *R.* v. *Muir* (1984) 79 Cr.App.R. 153 (C.A.). In that case, the accused's defence to a charge of a theft of a video tape recorder was that the machine had been repossessed by the company which had hired it to him. A district manager gave evidence that the local office had not repossessed the machine, and that he had telephoned head office and been told that there was no record there of a repossession. It was held that "in the way in which the evidence came out, it was admissible." So far as the investigation at branch office level is concerned, the reasoning appears to have been that the district manager was the best person to give the negative evidence which revealed that his office had none of the documentation which would be in existence in a repossession organised from that branch. It was accepted on behalf of the accused that the district manager could give evidence of the situation at his own branch. The district manager either had or was capable of having acquired personal knowledge of the absence of the relevant documents at his own branch, for he could investigate that question for himself. It is not easy, with respect, to see how the evidence of the telephone call to head office could be thought to stand in the same position. The fact that evidence of the call was elicited in cross-examination seems to have been crucial to the decision that the call should be treated as admissible. But the cross-examination was the direct outcome of the trial judge's ruling that the admissibility of a part of the *written* evidence of the district manager which related to the enquiries which he had made at head office (to which objection was taken on the ground that it was hearsay) should only be determined after the manager had given evidence of his system. The line of cross-examination adopted was a natural and logical one, perhaps a necessary one, as a result of the judge's failure to make a ruling at an earlier stage. In any event, the information obtained by the call cannot stand in the same position as the district manager's evidence as to the state of the records at his own office. In the case of the information emanating from head office, his evidence amounted to a statement that a third party had given him the informant that there was no documentation at head office. That being so, it was his information and not he who had the relevant knowledge. It is submitted that the evidence was therefore hearsay and inadmissible. The mere fact that it came out as a direct result of the defence adopting a particular line of cross-examination cannot, it is submitted, change its character or its admissibility. It might have been relevant if the defence had sought to rely on the fact that it had inadvertently been let in as a reason for stopping the trial and empanelling a new jury. This was not the position, and it is submitted that the evidence should have been excluded.

CHAPTER 17.—CIVIL EVIDENCE ACT 1968

(c) *Evidence other than first-hand hearsay*

17–07 1. *Documents produced by computers.* Add at end: *cf.* the simpler provisions contained in the Police and Criminal Evidence Act 1984, section 69.

17–08 2. *Documentary Records.* Add after NOTE 40: in order to satisfy the requirements of section 4(1), it is necessary that the records themselves be produced, and it is not enough to produce summaries of other records: *H.* v. *Schering Chemicals* [1983] 1 W.L.R. 143. Nor are the reports of inspectors appointed by the Department of Trade amounting as they do the secondary sources, documentary records: see *Savings and Investment Bank* v. *Gasco B.V.* [1984] 1 All E.R. 296.

(d) *Procedure*

17–12 NOTE 68. Add: the rules under the Civil Evidence Act make absence beyond the seas an unchallengeable justification for the admission of hearsay evidence, even though the relevant time appears to be the date of the notice rather than of the trial and irrespective of how easy it would be for the party to call him. (The Police and Criminal Evidence Act 1984 improves considerably on these provisions: see section 68(2)(a)(ii) which renders hearsay evidence admissible if the witness "is outside the U.K. and it is not reasonably practicable to secure his attendance.")

(e) *Discretion*

17–14 NOTE 88. Add: The provision was considered in *Greenaway* v. *Homelea Fittings* [1985] 1 W.L.R. 234, where it was held that a party was entitled to have the statement of an *ex*-employee excluded, partly because he was no longer in the party's employment, and partly because it would not be the best evidence. It was pointed out that though the former employers might call the man themselves, they would not automatically be entitled to treat him as a hostile witness.

(f) *Assessment*

17–16 Add after second sentence Note 99a. See the approach of Parker J. in *Bauche* v. *Woodhouse Drake* [1982] 2 Lloyd's Rep. 516 at 523. See also dicta of Brandon J. in *The Ferdinand Retzlaff* [1972] 2 Lloyd's Rep. 120 at 126–7 (which, with respect, expressed such an extreme scepticism as to the utility of hearsay evidence as to be at variance with the intent of the Act and with the modern cases on its scope, such as *Piermay* v. *Chester* (text 17–12)).

CHAPTER 18.—WRITTEN STATEMENTS IN CRIMINAL PROCEEDINGS

Criminal Evidence Act 1965

18–01 The Act has been repealed and replaced by the wider provisions of the Police and Criminal Evidence Act 1964.

Police and Criminal Evidence Act 1984

The law on documentary evidence in criminal proceedings has since January 1, 1986 been governed by Part VII of the Police and Criminal Evidence Act 1984. See Appendix to this supplement, *post* § 42–68 to 42–72 and § 42–83 to 42–85. Following the recommendation of the 11th Report of the Criminal Revision Committee in 1972, the 1984 Act moves towards assimilation of the rules for criminal and civil proceedings.

These provisions solve some, but not all, of the difficulties which arose under the 1965 Act. The Report of the Fraud Trials Committee (the Roskill Report), 1986, proposes wider admissibility of documents: paragraphs 5.9–5.19, 5.23–5.40.

The 1984 Act provides as follows:

Documentary records. Under section 68 and Schedule 3, a statement in a document is admissible as evidence of any fact stated therein of which direct oral evidence would be admissible, if both of two conditions are satisfied:

(a) that the document is or forms part of a record compiled by a person acting under a duty from information supplied by a person who had or may reasonably be supposed to have had personal knowledge of the matters dealt with (s.68(1)(a); and

(b) that the supplier of the information is unavailable or not to be called to give direct oral evidence for one of the reasons set out in section 68(2).

There is no provision requiring that notice be given to the other party of an intended use of hearsay evidence under section 68. However, in practice the prosecution will have served the document as part of their case. Moreover, a document falling within section 68(1) and prepared for the purpose of proceedings must be placed before the court and leave must be obtained before a statement in the document can be given in evidence: Schedule 3, paragraph 2. The court has a discretion, to be exercised in accordance with paragraph 2. Schedule 3, Parts I and III set out further detailed provisions, including guidance about inferences to be drawn in deciding on admissibility (paragraph 14) and about the weight to be attached to a statement in a document (paragraph 7).

Computer records. Under section 69 and Schedule 3 computer evidence is inadmissible unless it is shown that the computer was operating properly and was not likely to have produced an inaccurate statement because of improper use. Rules of Court may be made to provide for the form of the evidence. Schedule 3, Parts II and III set out various detailed provisions.

Microfilm copies. The contents of a document may be proved, even if the document itself is no longer in existence, by the production of an enlargement of a microfilm copy, authenticated in a manner approved by the court: s.71.

The Court of Appeal held that evidence was not hearsay and the 1965 Act did not apply in the following circumstances:

The defendant was indicted for the handling of three vehicle springs found on his premises. Records showed that the springs had been sent to the purchasers. The purchaser company records showed that the springs had been received into stock, had not been sold and that they were missing. The stock clerk and part sales manager of the purchaser company gave evidence that there was no record of the use or sale of the springs. It was submitted on appeal that this evidence was hearsay and that the evidence was not admissible under the Act. The Court of Appeal held that the evidence of the clerk and manager was not hearsay but was direct evidence from which the jury were entitled to infer that the springs were stolen: *R.* v. *Shone* (1983) 76 Cr.App.R. 72. The decision is not affected by the passing of the 1984 Act.

MAGISTRATES' COURTS ACT 1980

1. Depositions and Statements

(a) *Depositions taken under the Magistrates' Court Act* 1980, *s.*4 *and Magistrates' Courts Rules* 1981, *r.* 7

18–06 A statement should not be admitted under section 13(3) where it would be unfair to the defendant to do so: *R.* v. *Blithing* (1983) 77 Cr.App.R. 86. The court said that where a heavily prejudicial statement which could not be challenged in cross-examination was sought to be admitted, a plea for exclusion ought to succeed if the judge concluded that it would be unfair to a defendant to admit it.

MAGISTRATES' COURTS ACT 1980

Magistrates' Courts Act 1980, s.102

18–12 A *Practice Note* [1986] 2 All E.R. 511 has given detailed guidance on the preparation of and particularly on the editing of written statements.

ROAD TRAFFIC ACT 1972; READINGS OF MECHANICAL INSTRUMENTS GENERALLY

Under the Road Traffic Act 1972, section 10, as substituted by the Transport Act 1981, Schedule 8, certain "statements" and "certificates" are admissible as evidence of the proportion of alcohol or a drug in a specimen of breath, blood or urine (subject to compliance with the terms of the section). An alteration in handwriting will not necessarily prevent a statement from being a "statement automatically produced by the device" for the purposes of section 10(3): *Beck* v. *Scammell* [1986] R.T.R. 162 (D.C.). The "test record" document produced by a Lion Intoximeter 3000 breath testing device contains both a "statement" and a "certificate" within the meaning of the section; and a trained operator of the device may give evidence to explain the meaning of the "test record" contents: *Gaimster* v. *Marlow* [1984] Q.B. 218. Section 10(3) does not prevent the adducing or oral evidence: *Owen* v. *Chesters* [1985] Crim.L.R. 156. There is extensive case law on the section, outside the scope of a general work on evidence.

The test-record print-out of an automatic breath-testing device is in some circumstances admissible at common law, as real evidence: see *Castle* v. *Cross* [1985] 1 W.L.R. 1372 (D.C.), *ante* § 12–34, where the admissibility of mechanical instrument readings generally is considered.

CHAPTER 19.—ADMISSIONS

Rule

19–01 The general rule that admissions are only evidence against the party making them is sometimes forgotten. It was forgotten in *R.* v. *Spinks* [1982] 1 All E.R. 587; 74 Cr.App.R. 263. The defendant in that case was charged with assisting an offender contrary to Section 4(1) of the Criminal Law Act 1967 by concealing a knife which a co-defendant had used to wound another man. The prosecution had to prove that the co-defendant had committed an arrestable offence, namely wounding. The only evidence that such an offence had been committed was an admission by the co-defendant. A submission of no case was rejected and the defendant was convicted. The Court of Appeal quashed the conviction because the evidence of the co-defendant's admission was not admissible against the defendant and there was, as a consequence, no evidence that an arrestable offence had been committed. The Court of Appeal said that "the offence with which the appellant was charged and the means of establishing it do not provide any exception to the universal rule which excludes out of court admissions being used to provide evidence against a co-accused whether indicted jointly or separately" (74 Cr.App.R. 263, 266).

19–02 The law relating to the admissibility of confessions in criminal cases has been altered by the Police and Criminal Evidence Act 1984. See Chapter 22, *post*.

When and to whom admissions may be made

19–07 In criminal cases admissions by the defendant's agent are only admissible if it is proved that the admissions were made on the defendant's authority. In *R.* v. *Evans* [1981] Crim.L.R. 699 (a case concerning the handling of stolen goods), evidence was admitted of a conversation between a clerk of the defendant's solicitors and the defendant's brother-in-law. During the conversation the clerk said "the defendant has asked me to ask you to say that he bought the ring off you." The Court of Appeal held that the evidence was inadmissible. It could only have been admitted, if it had been proved that:

(i) the clerk had the defendant's authority to act,
(ii) the authority was established by evidence that the clerk and the defendant were jointly involved in a common enterprise,
(iii) that the clerk in speaking to the witness was acting in pursuance of the common purpose.

The court said that it was not enough that the clerk thought he was authorised or said that he was. Since the common purpose was not established, the evidence of the conversation was inadmissible. The authority of the agent must be established by admissible evidence. In this case the evidence of authority was hearsay (although it is scarcely conceivable that the clerk would have spoken as he did without the authority of the defendant). See also *R.* v. *Hutchinson, post*, § 19–08.

Circumstances of the admission

19–08 In *R.* v. *Hutchinson* [1985] Crim.L.R. 730, the Court of Appeal held that a statement by counsel at a pre-trial review in a criminal case was not admissible at the subsequent trial as an admission by the defendant. However, a letter from the defendant's solicitors to the D.P.P. was admissible where it contained an admission of presence at the scene of the crime, particularly because it contradicted an earlier alibi notice.

Offers "without prejudice"

19–10 NOTE 42. It has now been held by the Court of Appeal that letters containing offers to compromise made "without prejudice" but subject to an express reservation of the right to refer to the offer on the issue of costs are admissible in the question of costs: *Cutts* v. *Head and Another*, [1984] Ch. 290. The court noted that:

(a) in *Calderbank* v. *Calderbank* (1976) Fam. 93, 106, Cairns L.J. said that an offer to compromise a matrimonial dispute under sections 23 and 24 of the Matrimonial Causes Act 1973 might be made in the form that it was without prejudice to the issue at trial but reserved the right to refer to it on the issue of costs;

(b) there was a wide and continual practice in all divisions of the High Court to use letters in the above formula ("the *Calderbank* formula").

The Court said that it must now be taken as established that the *Calderbank* formula was not restricted to matrimonial proceedings but was available in all cases where a payment into court would be inappropriate.

19–11 NOTE 43. Add: *Norwich Union Life Insurance Society* v. *Tony Waller* (1984) 270 E.G. 42.

Whole statement must be taken, including hearsay and opinion

19–14 As to the effect of a "mixed" statement by a defendant in a criminal case, see *R.* v. *Duncan (Findlay)* (1981) 73 Cr.App.R. 359, § 33–60, *post*, in the text.

19–17 The mere fact that a defendant says that he believes goods are stolen does not relieve the prosecution of proving that the goods were stolen: *R.* v. *De Acetis, The Times,* January 22, 1982.

In cases of handling stolen goods, where it is sought to prove by admissions made by the accused that goods *were* stolen, a distinction must be made between statements made by the accused,

(a) as to his knowledge or belief that goods were stolen, based on what he had been told about them; and

(b) matters of fact reported from his own knowledge, *i.e.* matters of which he could give admissible evidence. Such matters might include the circumstances in which he came into possession of the goods and the price which he paid for them.

Statement (a) is relevant to prove the accused's state of knowledge or belief in relation to the goods. It does not go to prove that the goods were, *in fact*, stolen. The accused is reporting in this case a hearsay statement which may be inaccurate. Statement (b) is relevant to prove both the accused's state of knowledge and belief *and* to prove that the goods were stolen. In this case the accused is giving evidence of facts within his own knowledge (as opposed to reporting what he has been told). The jury may infer from what he says that the goods were stolen.

The above statement of the law is based on the dictum of Gibson J. in *R.* v.

Hulbert (1979) 69 Cr.App.R. 243, 246, 247 applied by the Court of Appeal in *R.* v. *Korniak* (1982) 76 Cr.App.R. 145. In the latter case Eveleigh L.J. said that a careful direction is often required in order to enable the jury to apply its mind to the relevant evidence on the particular issue.

Form of the admission

Conduct

19–23 In certain circumstances letters or oral statements which are not denied may be admissible as evidence of admission in criminal proceedings: *R.* v. *Edwards* [1983] Crim.L.R. 539; 80 L.S.Gaz. 1349, discussed at § 21–10, *infra*.

In *Preece and Ors.* v. *Parry* [1983] Crim.L.R. 170 the defendants created a disturbance in a public house. They then left in a van. When they had travelled about eight miles, the van was stopped by the police. The defendants were arrested. They were violent and abusive to the police. They were charged with offences contrary to section 5 of the Public Order Act 1936 in relation to their behaviour in the public house. At the trial in the magistrates' court, evidence of their behaviour on arrest was admitted. Their defence was that they had behaved peacefully in the public house. The defendants were convicted. On appeal the Divisional Court held that the evidence of the defendants' behaviour had been correctly admitted because it was inconsistent with the behaviour of innocent persons who had behaved peacefully in the public house and was reasonably capable of constituting an admission that the defendants had behaved in the way charged.

It is difficult to follow the reasoning in this case. A violent reaction to arrest is not an uncommon feature in cases. It is not necessarily an indication of guilt. It may simply be a reaction to the fact or shock of arrest or it may in some cases not be inconsistent with innocence. It may in certain circumstances be admissible as part of the *res gestae*. It may in other circumstances be admissible as similar fact evidence. It is difficult to see how in the circumstances of this case it can be said to amount to an *admission* of previous violent behaviour.

CHAPTER 20.—PERSONS WHOSE ADMISSIONS MAY BE EVIDENCE

Client, solicitor, counsel and witnesses

20–39 For the admissibility of an admission made by a solicitor's clerk in criminal proceedings, see *R.* v. *Evans* [1981] Crim.L.R. 699, § 19–07, *supra* in this supplement. See also *R.* v. *Hutchinson* [1985] Crim.L.R. 730, § 19–08, *supra.*

Counsel

20–40 Note 9. *Langdale* v. *Danby* is now reported at [1981] 1 W.L.R. 1123. See also *R.* v. *Hutchinson* [1985] Crim.L.R. 730, § 19–08, *supra.*

CHAPTER 21.—STATEMENTS IN THE PRESENCE, AND DOCUMENTS IN THE POSSESSION, OF A PARTY

2.—Documents

21–10 In *R.* v. *Edwards* [1983] Crim.L.R. 539, 80 L.S.Gaz. 1349, the Court of Appeal stated, that (a) in certain circumstances letters or oral statements which were not denied may be admissible in criminal cases as evidence of admission, but (b) the court must be very careful in admitting such evidence (Dictum of

Lord Esher M.R. in *Wiedemann* v. *Walpole* [1891] 2 Q.B. 534 at 537, 538 applied). In *R.* v. *Edwards*, the defendant was charged with inciting racial hatred by aiding the publication of a certain comic. A letter written to the defendant referring to the comic as "your idea and your work" was admitted as part of the prosecution case. An unfinished letter in reply found in the defendant's typewriter which did not refer to the comic was also admitted. The Court of Appeal doubted whether these letters were properly admitted. However the point was not decided since the court held that the direction as to their use by the jury was inadequate but applied the proviso.

The report of *R.* v. *Edwards* does not make it clear if the court said anything further as to the circumstances in which a letter would be admissible as evidence of admission. It is difficult to think of such circumstances. In the case of silence in the face of an accusation where a reply may properly be expected, the defendant is present and yet chooses to remain silent. Therefore the jury may infer guilt from the silence. In the case of a letter the failure to reply may be due to simple inertia.

CHAPTER 22.—CONFESSIONS AND THE ADMISSIBILITY OF EVIDENCE ILLEGALLY OBTAINED

Introductory: Police and Criminal Evidence Act 1984

The law in this chapter has been extensively altered by the Police and Criminal Evidence Act 1984. The relevant provisions came into force on January 1, 1986 and apply in trials commencing after that date. They are set out in the Appendix to this supplement, § 42–73 *et seq. post.*

The principal sections relevant to this chapter are as follows:

(1) Section 76 provides for the admissibility of confessions, in place of the common law rules: see *post*, § 22–03 to 22–10.

(2) Section 77 provides for a special need for caution in the case of confessions by mentally handicapped persons: see *post*, § 22–14.

(3) Section 78 provides for "the exclusion of unfair evidence": see *post*, § 22–48 to 22–55.

(4) Section 82(3) preserves the court's existing discretion to exclude evidence: see *post*, § 22–31 to 22–32.

Meaning of confession

22–01 For the purpose of a criminal case a confession "includes any statement wholly or partly adverse to the person who made it, whether made to a person in authority or not and whether in words or otherwise": Police and Criminal Evidence Act 1984, s.82(1).

Admissibility of confessions in criminal trials

22–02 This paragraph is unaffected by the Police and Criminal Evidence Act 1984.

Admissibility in law—principle

22–03 to 22–07 The test of admissibility stated in *Ibrahim* v. *R.* [1914] A.C. 599, at page 509, since extended to embrace "oppression," has been replaced by the statutory test in the Police and Criminal Evidence Act 1984, section 76.

A confession, in so far as it is relevant to any matter in issue, may be given in evidence in so far as it is not excluded: section 76(1). A confession is excluded if the prosecution fails to prove (if required to do so) that the confession was not obtained

"(a) by oppression of the person who made it; or

"(b) in consequence of anything said or done which was likely, in the circumstances existing at the time, to render unreliable any confession which might be made by him in consequence thereof": s.76(2).

"Oppression" is defined by section 76(8) as including "torture, inhuman or degrading treatment, and the use or threat of violence (whether or not amounting to torture)".

Where there is oppression, the confession is excluded if obtained by that oppression and the court is not required to consider whether the oppression was likely to render the confession unreliable. It is submitted that not every use of force (for example, the forcible application of handcuffs) will necessarily amount to "violence" for the purposes of section 76(2).

The statutory definition of "oppression" is not exhaustive. It seems to follow that the courts should continue to apply their own description of oppression as "something which tends to sap, and has sapped, that free will which must exist before a confession is voluntary": see *R.* v. *Prager* (1972) 56 Cr.App.R. 151 and the test at § 22–06. The same reasoning was used in such cases (prior to the 1984 Act) as *R.* v. *Gowan and others* [1982] Crim.L.R. 821. In *R.* v. *Gardner*, reported only in [1986] 7 C.L. 143, H.H. Judge Lymbery Q.C. held on May 1, 1986, after the 1984 Act came into force, that "it had to be established beyond reasonable doubt that the answers were made voluntarily, namely not under oppression." Thus it seems likely that "voluntariness" may remain a matter to be considered under the first limb of section 76(2).

Under the second limb of the sub-section, the test is entirely new. The court first considers whether anything was said or done which was likely, in the circumstances existing at the time, to render unreliable any confession made in consequence. If something was so said or done, the court then considers whether the confession was in fact obtained in consequence thereof. The court is not directed to consider whether the confession is in fact unreliable. Section 76(2) requires the exclusion of a confession "notwithstanding that it may be true."

In considering whether a confession was obtained "in consequence" of what was said or done, the court may have to embark on an exercise similar to the exercise of considering whether a confession was voluntary. It is submitted, however, that it is unhelpful to refer to "voluntariness" in reaching decisions under section 76(2). Very few confessions are voluntary in the sense that they are volunteered without the process of arrest and questioning. As the Court of Appeal pointed out in *R.* v. *Rennie* [1982] 1 W.L.R. 64, at page 69, very few confessions are inspired solely by remorse. *Rennie* is fully discussed in the text at § 22–22. The courts are now freed by section 76(2) from having to consider whether there was a "fear or prejudice or hope of advantage exercised or held out by a person in authority" and whether the confession was therefore not voluntary. Threats and promises are of course examples of things said or done which may require consideration under section 76(2). They are no more than examples. The court is directed by the sub-section to concentrate on the likely effect on the reliability of the confession. Such a likelihood is a rational basis for a decision on admissibility, even if it inevitably depends crucially on the judgment of the particular judge.

Apart from the discussion of the term "oppression" in § 22–06, the text in paragraphs 22–03 to 22–07 must be regarded as superseded.

22–08 The burden remains on the prosecution of proving that the confession was not obtained by means that would make it inadmissible. Proof is required beyond reasonable doubt. See section 76(2) and (3). (Although section 76(3) does not mention proof beyond reasonable doubt, it would produce an astonishing result to conclude that the omission is significant).

Paragraph 22–08 in the text must be regarded as superseded.

Procedure

22–09 to 22–10 Section 76 provides some guidance on procedure. If it is represented to the court that the confession was or may have been obtained by the means referred to in section 76(2), then the court, that is, the judge, must rule: s.76(2). The court may of its own motion require the prosecution to discharge the necessary burden of proof before the confession is admitted. It must follow that in either event a voire dire will be held before the confession is "given in evidence."

Subject to noting that the test of admissibility is different, the law stated in paragraph 22–09 is still good law.

It was held prior to the Act that a trial within a trial is not an appropriate procedure when a case is conducted before magistrates, there being no point in doing so because the magistrates are judges of both fact and law: *F. (An Infant)* v. *Chief Constable of Kent* [1982] Crim.L.R. 682. Thus although, as the court held, it was appropriate to decide such an incidental matter as a separate issue, there was no need to have evidence already heard for that purpose repeated during the main trial. Section 76(2) does not readily fit summary proceedings, because a confession may have to be "given in evidence" for the purpose of the section 76 issue. It would surely nevertheless be an artificial exercise for the confession to be given in evidence again after magistrates had heard the evidence and ruled that it was admissible.

In *R.* v. *Hay* (1983) 77 Cr.App.R. 70, it was held that a defendant was entitled to adduce evidence of an earlier acquittal in a trial in which the prosecution relied on the same confession as in the instant case. The 1984 Act would appear not to affect that principle.

In *R.* v. *Pervez and Khan* [1983] Crim.L.R. 108, applications for separate trials were granted after confession statements were ruled admissible. At subsequent trials the judge refused to consider admissibility afresh. The Court of Appeal upheld his refusal. Again, the 1984 Act would appear not to affect the reasoning involved.

It is more difficult to say whether section 76 affects the principles laid down in *Ajodha* v. *The State* (1981) 73 Cr.App.R. 129 (P.C.), discussed fully in § 22–10 in the text.

Three cases prior to the 1984 Act require consideration first. In *R.* v. *Cunningham* [1985] Crim.L.R. 374, the defendant in his evidence made an allegation of inducement against two police officers who had not been called by the prosecution. On a submission of no case at the end of his evidence, the prosecution applied successively to call the two officers in rebuttal, despite the fact that cross-examination during the prosecution case had alerted the prosecution to the likelihood that the allegation would be made. The Court of Appeal, dismissing an appeal against conviction, stated that the discretion to allow the rebuttal evidence had been correctly exercised. The Court also hoped that a voir dire would usually be used. In *R.* v. *Airey*, [1985] Crim.L.R. 305 the Court of Appeal confirmed that a defendant was entitled to take advantage of the alternative *Ajodha* procedure and postpone the submission until both judge and jury had heard the evidence. In *R.* v. *Jackson* [1985] Crim.L.R. 444, the Court of Appeal described the voir dire as the normal procedure.

Section 76(2) obviously permits the defendant to require a voir dire. Section 76(3) states that the court "may of its own motion" require the prosecution to prove that the confession is admissible as a condition of allowing the confession to be given in evidence. It appears that section 76(2) permits the prosecution to represent to the judge that the confession "may" have been obtained by means prohibited by section 76(2). That representation would oblige the court to rule; there may be cases in which the prosecution prefer to have an issue they see as likely to arise decided at an early stage. What is not clear is whether in the latter situation the defence can require the voir dire to take place in the presence of the jury or whether, more importantly, the defence can postpone making representations until after the evidence has been heard. The difficulty arises because section 76(2) contemplates the raising of the issue before the confession is "given in evidence." The section does not deal with the situation where the evidence is heard by the jury before any question of admissibility is raised.

The point remains to be authoritatively resolved. It is likely that section 76(2) will make the courts encourage the use of the voir dire, particularly in the light of the attitudes expressed in *Cunningham* and *Jackson, supra*. Judges may well use section 76(3) to require a voir dire. However, it remains at least doubtful whether the court has power to require the jury to withdraw unless the defence consent: *R.* v. *Anderson* (1929) 21 Cr.App.R. 178. Moreover, if any evidence, including a confession, is given and later is shown to be inadmissible, a judge must surely as a matter of general principle take appropriate action. Such action may be a direction to the jury to ignore the evidence or (if there is no other evidence) a ruling that there is no case to answer or even in an appropriate case the exercise of the discretion to discharge the jury.

Thus *Ajodha* is probably still good law, subject to the qualifications just mentioned.

The rule that in the voir dire the defendant may not be asked in cross-examination questions as to the truth of the alleged confession appears to be preserved by section 76(2).

See further: Peter Rowe, The Voire Dire and the Jury [1986] Crim.L.R. 226.

The admissibility of evidence given in the voir dire in the substantive trial

22–11 to 22–13 The law stated in these paragraphs is not affected by the Police and Criminal Evidence Act 1984.

Function of judge and jury

22–14 This paragraph must be read with the new test of admissibility in mind. In § 22–03 to 22–07, *supra*. However, it must remain the situation that if a judge rules that a confession is admissible, the jury may have to consider the circumstances in which a statement was made in order to assess whether it is true.

The 1984 Act makes one change. Section 77 requires a judge to warn the jury of a special need for caution in a case in which the case against a mentally handicapped person depends wholly or substantially on a confession and the confession was not made in the presence of an independent person. Section 77 further defines the relevant terms, deals with the burden of proof in certain circumstances and provides for summary trials.

Matters probable by confession

22–15 The law stated in this paragraph remains unaffected by the Police and Criminal Evidence Act 1984.

Use and misuse of confessions by prosecution

22–16 to 22–17 The law stated in paragraph 22–16 is not affected by the Police and Criminal Evidence Act 1984. Paragraph 22–17 also remains good law, subject to the effect of section 74 on the evidential value of the conviction of others.

Section 76(4)(b) provides that a confession may be admissible for the purpose of showing that the accused speaks, writes or expresses himself in a particular way. This is so even if the confession is excluded under section 76 for other purposes. However, for the purpose of section 76(4)(*b*) only so much of the confession as is necessary for that purpose is admissible. It is obvious that a judge would "be likely to" exercise his discretion to exclude any part of a confession for this purpose if the effect would be to place before the jury the fact that the defendant had confessed.

In *R.* v. *Rowson and others* [1985] 3 W.L.R. 99, the Court of Appeal held that where a statement made by a defendant is ruled to be inadmissible, he may nevertheless be cross-examined on the statement on behalf of a co-defendant if he gives evidence inconsistent with the statement. It is submitted that the decision is unaffected by the passing of the 1984 Act.

Persons in authority

22–18 to 22–19 The law about who is a person in authority, with all its technicalities, is swept away by section 76 of the Police and Criminal Evidence Act 1984. The fact that something was said or done by a person in authority will of course be one of the circumstances that may be relevant to a judge considering section 76, but it is no more than that.

The inducement

22–20 The technicalities of the law on inducements are also swept away by the 1984 Act. It does not matter whether what is "said or done" is or is not an inducement; the test in section 76(2)(*b*) is not dissimilar, but references to what has been held to be an inducement will be unhelpful.

Use of previous decisions

22–21 The warning given in *D.P.P.* v. *Ping Lin* [1976] A.C. 574 (H.L.) (see text) is at least as apposite in reaching decisions on section 76(2). Unless a previous decision establishes some principle on the construction of section 76, the citation of decisions on different, or even similar, facts will be unhelpful. Section 76 requires consideration on the likely effect "on him," that is, on the particular defendant.

R. v. Rennie

22–22 The difficulties to which *Rennie* was addressed have been removed (even if others have been introduced) by the Police and Criminal Evidence Act 1984, section 76.

The subject matter of the inducement

22–23 to 22–25 What is said, *ante*, in § 22–20, applies equally to these paragraphs.

Removal of the inducement or the caution

22–26 The law in this paragraph is superseded by the Police and Criminal Evidence Act 1984, although similar considerations will arise under the Act. A judge considering section 76 must consider whether the confession was obtained *by* oppression or *in consequence of* anything said or done likely to render the confession unreliable. If lapse of time or intervening events remove the effect of what would otherwise lead to the exclusion of the confession, the prosecution will have proved that the confession was "not obtained as aforesaid" (s.76(2)).

Admissions under compulsory process of law

22–27 This section of the text is not affected by the Police and Criminal Evidence Act 1984.

22–28 The Companies Act 1967, section 50, is now replaced by the Companies Act 1985, section 434(5) (as to answers to questions) and the Insolvency Act 1985, section 231 (as to the statement of affairs). The power to appoint inspectors is now to be found in the Companies Act 1985, section 431 *et seq.*

Confessions induced by persons not in authority

22–30 Under the Police and Criminal Evidence Act 1984, section 76, it does not matter whether the actions relied on under (2)(*a*) or (*b*) are those of persons in authority or not. The status of the person is simply one of the circumstances that may be relevant.

Discretion to exclude confession admissible in law

22–31 to 22–32 The Police and Criminal Evidence Act 1984 contains three relevant provisions:

(1) Section 82(3) preserves any existing discretion of the court to exclude evidence "whether by preventing questions from being put or otherwise."

(2) Section 78(1) introduces a new discretion: The court may exclude evidence "if it appears to the court that, having regard to all the circumstances, including the circumstances in which the evidence was obtained, the admission of the evidence would have such an adverse effect on the fairness of the proceedings that the court ought not to admit it."

(3) The Codes of Practice issued under section 66 of the Act are admissible in evidence in all criminal and civil proceedings; "and if any provision of such a code appears to the court or tribunal conducting the proceedings to be relevant to any question arising in the proceedings it shall be taken into account in determining that question": section 67(11). The Codes supersede the Judges' Rules and are considered in more detail in § 22–33 to 22–38, *post.*

In relation to confessions it may well be that section 78(1) largely, if not entirely, supersedes the discretion described in *R.* v. *Sang* (1979) 69 Cr.App.R. 282 to exclude a confession obtained by improper or unfair means. Nevertheless, because section 82(3) preserves any existing discretion, it may be necessary for courts to consider whether *Sang* gives rise to exclusion even if section 78(1) does not. The distinction may be somewhat artificial. However, the final words of section 78(1) place on the defendant arguing for exclusion the burden of persuading the court that the adverse effect would be sufficient. Hitherto courts which have found a breach of the Judges' Rules or some equivalent breach have spoken in terms of whether to exercise their discretion to admit the evidence, effectively placing on the prosecution the burden of persuasion. See, for example, *R.* v. *Marsh* [1985] Crim.L.R. 47 (Central Criminal Court). It is submitted that it would be more satisfactory to regard section 78(1) as the sole basis for the exercise of the court's discretion to exclude admissible confessions, except in those rare cases where a confession is excluded because its prejudicial effect outweights its probative value. The latter general discretion is obviously preserved by section 82(3).

Courts will be invited to exercise the discretion to exclude confessions because of some breach of the Codes of Practice. However, such Codes are admissible by virtue of section 67(11), if relevant, during the court's consideration of admissibility under section 76(2). If in a particular case a breach of a Code does not amount to oppression and is not likely to render the confession unreliable, it may be that only rarely will the discretion be exercised to exclude the confession. This may be the effect of enacting a more rational test of admissibility in section 76(2).

It is interesting to compare *R.* v. *Miller* [1986] 3 All E.R. 119 (C.A.), decided under the old law. The defendant, a paranoid schizophrenic, made a confession which included delusionary material. The judge held that on the facts there was no oppression and exercised his discretion to admit the confession. The appeal against conviction was dismissed. The decision would be likely to be the same now. In the absence of oppression or anything said or done likely to render a confession unreliable, the confession would be admissible. There would be a discretion to exclude the confession if made in a state of delusion, because section 78(1) provides for all the circumstances to be considered. Nevertheless, where on the facts (as in *Miller*) there was a basis for the jury to distinguish between rational and irrational parts, the judge would be likely not to exclude it.

For section 78, see further § 22–48 to 22–55.

The Judges' Rules. The Police and Criminal Evidence Act and the Codes of Practice

22–33 to 22–38 The Judge's Rules have been superseded, in part by provisions of the Police and Criminal Evidence Act itself and in part by the Codes of Practice issued under section 66. The Act and the Codes contain very detailed provisions for the arrest, detention and questioning of suspects. A court may obviously have to consider such provisions in reaching decisions on admissibility of confessions and on the exercise of the discretion to exclude confessions. Section 67(11) expressly requires a Code to be taken into account if relevant to any question that arises for determination.

It does not of course follow that breach of the Act or a Code is necessarily significant for present purposes. Some provisions are designed for the decent treatment of suspects, or their safety, but may have no possible relevance to the reliability of a confession or the fairness of the proceedings. Some provisions are important in ensuring that the confession is accurately recorded, but not important on the question of admissibility.

The provisions that may be most relevant for present purposes are listed here for convenience:

(1) Arrest. Act, ss.24–25, 28–32.

(2) Detention. Act, ss.34–48. Code of Practice for the Detention Treatment and Questioning of Persons by Police Officers (Code C), 1.1–4.5, 8.1–9.9, 16.1–16.5, Annex E.

(3) Communication with persons outside the police station; legal advice. Act, ss.56–58. Code C, 5.1–7.7 and Annex B.

(4) Questioning. Act, s.60. Code C, 10.1–15.2, Annexes C and D. See

especially 10.1 *et seq.* (cautions), 11.1 to 13.3 and Annex C (interviews) and Annex D (written statements under caution).

A defendant may not be cross-examined about his reasons for refusing to answer questions from police after he has been cautioned: *W.* v. *Boothby*, The Times, July 4, 1986 (D.C.).

Breach of the Judges' Rules

22–39 See § 22–33 to 22–38, *ante*, for the effect of a breach of the Codes which replace the Judges' Rules.

The effect of *Sang* on breach of the Judges' Rules

22–40 See § 22–33 to 22–38, *ante*, for the effect of a breach of the Codes which replace the Judges' Rules.

Other Administrative Directions

22–41 to 22–42 The Administrative Directions annexed to the Judges' Rules have also been replaced by the Police and Criminal Evidence Act 1984 and the Codes issued thereunder. Section 62 of the Criminal Law Act 1977 has been replaced by more detailed provisions in section 56 of the 1984 Act. See § 22–33 to 22–38, *ante*, for the effect of breach of the 1984 Act and of the Codes.

Form of confession

22–43 The law in this paragraph is not altered by the partial definition of "confession" in the Police and Criminal Evidence Act 1984, section 82(1).

The Code of Practice for the Detention, Treatment and Questioning of Persons by Police Officers (Code C) makes provisions for interview records (11.3 to 11.7) and other documentation in relation to interviews (12.9 to 12.15). See also Annex D of the Code (written statements under caution).

Section 60 of the 1984 Act provides for the issue of a code of practice for the tape-recording of interviews and for the making of an order requiring tape-recording of interviews. No steps have yet been taken under section 60, but a draft code of practice has been issued and trials of tape-recording have been in progress in several areas. In those areas many interviews are being tape-recorded and such tape-recording, and the preparation of evidence for court proceedings, is conducted in accordance with local detailed schemes and police operational orders. The latter have no statutory force and are not binding on courts, but are of practical importance to those conducting proceedings.

Whole confession admissible

22–44 The law in this paragraph is not affected by the Police and Criminal Evidence Act 1984. Section 76(1) permits the editing of parts of a confession by using the words "a confession . . . may be given in evidence . . . in so far as it is relevant . . . ."

Section 76(4) permits the use of part of an inadmissible confession to show that the accused speaks, writes or expresses himself in a particular way. See § 22–16 to 22–17, *ante*.

For the effect of a "mixed" statement which includes exculpatory parts, see *R.* v. *Duncan (Findley)* (1981) 73 Cr.App.R. 359 and § 33–60 in the text.

Ambiguous confessions

22–45 The law in this paragraph is not affected by the Police and Criminal Evidence Act 1984.

To, and by, whom confessions may be made

22–46 to 22–47 Section 82(1) of the Police and Criminal Evidence Act 1984 enacts in terms that a confession includes a statement "whether made to a person in authority or not." Subject to the new test of admissibility of a confession, the 1984 Act does not alter the law stated in these paragraphs.

Admissibility of evidence obtained in consequence of (a) an unlawful act; (b) an inadmissible confession

(a) *Evidence obtained as a consequence of an unlawful act*

22–48 to 22–54 The Police and Criminal Evidence Act 1984, section 82(3) preserves the court's existing discretion to exclude evidence. It must follow that in so far as *R.* v. *Sang* (1979) 69 Cr.App.R. 282 (H.L.) permits the court to exclude evidence in its discretion, that discretion survives.

Section 78(1) provides a new discretion. The sub-section is set out at § 22–31 to 22–32, *ante*. (See also the discussion in those paragraphs).

Section 78(1) is a difficult sub-section. It plainly provides for three stages. First, the court must "have regard to all the circumstances, including the circumstances in which the evidence was obtained." Secondly, the sub-section requires the court to consider whether the admission of the evidence would have such an adverse effect on the fairness of the proceedings that the court ought not to admit it." Thirdly, the court must exercise its discretion.

The sub-section was considered by McCullough J. in *R.* v. *Ranuana and Others* (unreported), Birmingham Crown Court, October 1986, when he rejected a submission that evidence allegedly obtained by the action of an agent provocateur should be excluded. McCullough J. doubted the correctness of the prosecution's concession that the words "including the circumstances in which the evidence was obtained" could apply to evidence so obtained; he doubted whether the Act can have been intended, even in rare circumstances, effectively to provide the defendant with a defence of entrapment, a defence not known to the law.

Dealing with the first stage, McCullough J. did not finally resolve the question on whom the burden of proof lies, nor what is the standard of proof. He pointed out the undesirability of a judge making findings that might in effect be the very decisions a jury would be required to make. He also pointed out the difficulty of reaching firm conclusions at such a preliminary stage. In the event, having heard such evidence as the parties invited him to hear, he made findings where possible and took into account possibilities where no firm conclusion was possible.

McCullough J. also pointed out that if a conclusion adverse to the evidence was reached at the second stage, that conclusion effectively decided which way the court's discretion should be exercised.

The sub-section awaits further authoritative interpretation. Its scope is very wide: "all the circumstances" are to be considered. The "circumstances in which the evidence was obtained" are not limited by the sub-section and appear to include circumstances both of illegality and any other kind of impropriety. However, since the evidence being considered will be both relevant and admissible, the occasions on which a court reaches a conclusion at the second stage adverse to the evidence are likely to be rare. A very real difficulty arises at the first stage if there is a dispute about the "circumstances." It may be that a court at that stage should not find facts, but simply look at the circumstances as they appear to be at the time of the court's ruling; if there is doubt about some relevant matter, the existence of that doubt is one of the "circumstances" to which the court must have regard.

In *R.* v. *Apicella* [1986] Crim.L.R. 238 (C.A.) it was held, prior to the 1984 Act, that evidence that the defendant suffered from gonorrhoea was rightly admitted. He had submitted to a sample being taken in prison for the purpose of treatment. Although the court stressed that the law under the 1984 Act was not being considered, the court did say "The pertinent question was whether the intended use of the evidence was likely to make the trial unfair." These words seem to indicate that the court was considering a discretion to exclude in addition to the question of admissibility.

In *Fox* v. *Chief Constable of Gwent* [1985] 1 W.L.R. 1126 (H.L.) it was held, prior to the 1984 Act, that evidence of excess alcohol obtained in accordance with the Road Traffic Act 1972, as amended, and without any inducement, threat, trick, or other impropriety, was not rendered inadmissible merely because the defendant had been unlawfully arrested. See also *Gull* v. *Scarborough, The Times*, November 15, 1985 (Div.Ct).

22–55 NOTE 25a. *Helliwell* v. *Piggott Sims* is reported at [1980] F.S.R. 356.

(b) *Evidence obtained as a consequence of an inadmissible confession*

22–56 to 22–57 The law is now statutory. The Police and Criminal Evidence Act, 1984, section 76(4)(a) provides that the whole or partial exclusion of a confession shall not affect the admissibility in evidence of any facts discovered as a result of the confession. Moreover, evidence that a fact was discovered as a result of an excluded confession or excluded part of a confession is not admissible "unless evidence of how it was discovered is given by him or on his behalf": s.76(4), (5). On a strict interpretation of these sub-sections, the prosecution could cross-examine the defendant on the point in order that evidence "is given by him." However, if that strict interpretation is indeed correct, a court would no doubt in its discretion prevent such a circumvention of the rest of the section.

CHAPTER 23.—RES GESTAE: SPONTANEOUS STATEMENTS AS EXCEPTION TO THE HEARSAY RULE

Ratten v. R.

23–09 In *R.* v. *Turnbull* (1985) 80 Cr.App.R. 104 the Court of Appeal considered the words "concoction or distortion" in the speech of Lord Wilberforce cited in the text, and held that the meaning of distortion in that context was adaptation, "adapt[ing] the matter in a way favourable to himself and antagonistic to another," and not in the sense that there was a distorted account of what had been said. Evidence was admitted that a dying man, asked who had stabbed him, said "Ronnie Tommo"; it was the prosecution's case that the second word was an attempt by the deceased, with a thick Scottish accent and after drinking a great deal, to say "Turnbull."

CHAPTER 24.—COMMON LAW EXCEPTIONS TO THE RULE AGAINST HEARSAY: STATEMENTS BY DECEASED PERSONS

2.—DECLARATIONS AGAINST INTEREST

The interest

24–12 NOTE 38. The reference to *R.* v. *O'Brien* should have been to 5 W.W.R.; and see now (1978) 76 D.L.R. (3d) 513.

3.—DECLARATIONS IN THE COURSE OF DUTY

Criminal proceedings

The duty

24–26 NOTE 6. In *R.* v. *McGuire* [1985] Crim.L.R. 663 the Court of Appeal held that while the factual parts of the report of a deceased scientific officer were admissible, those parts of the report expressing opinion were not.

CHAPTER 25.—COMMON LAW EXCEPTIONS TO THE RULE AGAINST HEARSAY: STATEMENTS IN PUBLIC OR OFFICIAL DOCUMENTS AND CORPORATION BOOKS

6.—CORPORATION, COMPANY AND BANKERS' BOOKS

Bankers' Books

25–82 Letters contained in a bank correspondence file have been held not to be bankers' books within the meaning of section 9 of the Bankers' Books Evidence Act 1879: *R.* v. *Dadson* (1983) 77 Cr.App.R. 91.

Section 9 of the Bankers' Books Evidence Act has now been substituted by paragraphs 1 and 13 of schedule 6 to the Banking Act 1973. The new section 9 is set out in the text.

25–84 *Inspection. Williams* v. *Summerfield* for which the correct reference is [1972] 2 Q.B. 512, was applied in *R.* v. *Nottingham City Justices, ex p. Lynn* (1984) 79 Cr.App.R. 238 (D.C.). The court will not, save in exceptional circumstances, require the production on subpoena or order under the Bankers' Books Evidence Act 1897 of documents outside the jurisdiction concerning business transacted outside it: *McKinnon* v. *Donaldson and Others* [1986] 2 W.L.R. 453.

CHAPTER 27.—REPUTATION, OPINION, INFERENCE, BELIEF

2.—EXCEPTIONS

(b) *Opinions of Experts*

27–07 NOTE 44. In *R.* v. *Abadom* (1983) 76 Cr.App.R. 48 (C.A.), particles of glass found in the accused's shoes were identical in composition to the glass broken in the course of a burglary. An expert witness, basing his opinion on statistics collected by others, expressed the view that there was only a four per cent. chance of such an identity being found in two pieces of glass. *English Exporters (London) Ltd.* v. *Eldonwall* (see text) was followed, and the evidence held admissible. (The rule is too narrowly expressed in the text.) In *R.* v. *Bradshaw* [1985] 82 Cr.App.R. 79 (C.A.), it was held that a doctor can give evidence of what a patient told him in order to explain the basis of his diagnosis; but that did not amount to evidence that the patient in fact suffered from the symptoms so described. See also *H.* v. *Schering Chemicals* [1983] 1 W.L.R. 143; and for an article dealing with this topic, see "Expert Opinion Evidence Based on Hearsay," Rosemary Pattenden [1982] Crim.L.R. 85.

27–08 Add at end: the suggestion in the text that there is a difference between expert evidence of fact and expert evidence of opinion has been confirmed in *The Torenia* [1983] 2 Lloyd's Rep. 210, 233, although in that case no practical consequences followed from the holding.

27–09 Add at end: while the statements of fact contained in records made contemporaneously by persons acting under a duty are admissible, the expert opinions they formed are not. They are not spontaneous and not mechanical, not subject to routine checking, nor is it impossible to obtain other evidence. Thus in *R.* v. *McGuire* (1985) 81 Cr.App.R. 323 (C.A.) the notes of a scientific expert made after a fire were admitted, but his report excluded. (It is thought, however, that there will be cases where the reliability of the expert's record of the facts or the exact nature of his observations can be fairly ascertained only by reference to the opinions he expresses, even though the opinion itself is not evidence of its own validity.)

27–10 NOTE 62. Add: see Harnon, "Evidence Obtained By Polygraph: an Israeli Perspective" [1982] Crim.L.R. 340 (of more general interest than the title might indicate).

NOTE 63. Add: for a less enthusiastic view of evidence obtained by hypnosis, see "Hypnosis and the Law: a Critical Review of Some Recent Proposals," Wagstaff [1983] Crim.L.R. 152.

27–11 NOTES 64–70. Add: *R.* v. *Masih* [1986] Crim.L.R. 395 (C.A.). Evidence which showed the accused to have been on the border between dull normality and subnormality was held to have been rightly excluded, because the defendant was normal, even if only by a small margin. All questions about his mental capacity were therefore for the jury not for psychiatric experts. *R.* v. *Turner* (see text) was followed, and *R.* v. *Chard* (see text) was held to have added nothing to that decision. *R.* v. *Lowery* (see text) was said to have been a decision on special facts; and the Australian case of *Schultz* v. *R.* [1981] W.A.R. 171 to have gone too far.

NOTE 70a. *R.* v. *Mackenney and Pinfold* (1983) 76 Cr.App.R. 271 (C.A.). It is for the jury to decide whether or not the accused is telling lies, and expert evidence that he is the type of man who *may* tell lies is inadmissible. See also *R.* v. *Rimmer and Beech* [1983] Crim.L.R. 250 (C.A.) and *R.* v. *Neale* (1977) 64 Cr.App.R. 304 (C.A.). On the topic of expert evidence on matters of psychology, see an article by Anthony Kenny, "The Expert in Court" (1983) 99 L.Q.R. 197.

27–12 NOTE 74. Add: Assessors were appointed after the hearing in *Esso* v. *Southport Corp.* [1956] A.C. 218 (see *per* Devlin J. at 222–3), but the learned judge observed that it would not normally be the practice to employ assessors who had not been present at the trial.

Scope: grounds and form of the opinion: hypothetical questions

27–14 NOTE 91. Add: but see above § 27–07, NOTE 44.

(ii) Civil Proceedings

27–19 NOTE 15. Add: see *Ollett* v. *Bristol Aerojet* [1979] 1 W.L.R. 1197n.

Add after sub-paragraph (a)(iii): (iv) it is immaterial, so far as the applicability of the rules of court are concerned whether the expert evidence is of fact or opinion. In either case, the appropriate notice must be served: *The Torenia* [1983] 2 Lloyd's Rep. 210, 233. (v) The fact that the expert evidence is to be given by a party to the action does not exonerate him from the duty to disclose his report: *Shell Pensions Trust* v. *Pell Frischmann* [1986] 2 All E.R. 911.

27–19A Add after § 27–19. In *The Marion* [1982] 2 Lloyd's Rep. 52, one party sought leave to tender expert evidence out of time, and after objection it was ruled that only the witness's evidence of fact would be admitted. The other party later sought himself to rely on the expert's report, praying in aid R.S.C. Ord. 38, r. 42, but it was *held* that they were not entitled to do so because the report had not been "disclosed . . . in accordance with this part of this Order."

27–20 Add: Note 22a. For an even more extreme expression of the same attitude, see *Kelly* v. *L.J.E.* [1982] 1 W.L.R. 1055 (C.A.). Note 25. Add Kenny *op. cit., supra* § 27–11 Notes 64–70.

27–23 Notes 36–37. Add: *Ollett* v. *Bristol Aerojet* (*supra* § 27–19), an important Practice direction as to the mode of report which satisfies the Rules.

27–24 Note 42. *Hinds* v. *London Transport Executive* is reported at [1978] R.T.R. 103. The decision was distinguished in *Sullivan* v. *West Yorkshire Passenger Transport Executive* [1985] 2 All E.R. 134 (C.A.) where it was held that it was not up to the Master to decide whether or not expert evidence was admissible. It was said that the *Hinds* case was different because it was an application under R.S.C. Ord. 38, r. 40, rather than Ord. 38 r. 38 as in *Sullivan*'s case; but the distinctions drawn are extremely unconvincing.

(a) Oral medical evidence

27–26 Note 44. For R.S.C. Ord. 38, r. 37(1), read Ord. 38, r. 37(2) and add: *Kirkup* v. *British Rail Engineering Ltd.* [1983] 1 W.L.R. 190 (C.A.), which holds that it is not necessary that there be a simultaneous exchange of reports in every case. In an appropriate case, the Plaintiff could be required, as he was in this case, to disclose his report in advance to the defendants, so that the latter and their expert might know what was the particular medical case the defendants had to meet.

This procedure was held to be exceptional in *Aston* v. *Firth Brown* [1984] 6 C.L. 142, where it was said that it was caused by the fact that the Plaintiff's claim was inadequately pleaded and because there were thousands of similar cases against the Defendants around the country. In *Aston*'s case (also a case on industrial deafness) it was held that the party who disclosed in advance would be at a disadvantage, and, absent exceptional circumstances, the normal order for mutual disclosure would be followed.

Note 45. For R.S.C. Ord. 38, r. 37(2) read Ord. 38, r. 37(3).

Note 46. Add: *Brown* v. *Merton Health Authority* [1982] 1 All E.R. 650 (C.A.) confirms that there should not normally be disclosure ordered of medical reports relating to the issue of negligence on the part of medical practitioners. Moreover, where there is no issue on the pleadings as to such negligence, no expert evidence should be permitted in any event.

Note 47. Add *Kirkup* v. *British Rail Engineering Ltd.* (*supra*), which holds that the two cases specified in Ord. 38, r. 37(2) are not exclusive.

Note 49. Add: See *Brown* v. *Merton Health Authority* (*supra*, Note 46) for the ordinary form of order relating to disclosure of reports relating to the medical condition and prognosis of an injured plaintiff.

27–31 Add at end of Paragraph. New procedures have been introduced by the Police and Criminal Evidence Act 1984. By section 81, it is provided that Rules of Court may be made by the Crown Court (but *not* by magistrates' courts) for requiring disclosure of experts' reports and for prohibiting the adduction of expert evidence by persons who fail to comply.

(iv) Competency and credit

27–32 NOTE 76. Add: *R.* v. *Mackenney and Pinfold* (1973) 76 Cr.App.R. 271 (C.A.), where some departure from the laxity referred to in the text was undertaken, and a man with qualifications in social anthropology and social psychology was held not qualified to give evidence about a person's state of mind, because he was not a psychiatrist. See also Kenny, *op. cit. supra* § 27–20.

(v) Compellability of expert witnesses

27–33 NOTE 88. Add: *R.* v. *King* [1983] 1 W.L.R. 411 (C.A.).

(vi) Value of expert evidence

27–34 NOTE 90. Add: *R.* v. *Vernege* [1982] Crim.L.R. 598 (C.A.), *R.* v. *Byrne* [1960] 2 Q.B. 396 at 402; *R.* v. *Dix* (1982) 74 Cr.App.R. 306 (C.A.); *R.* v. *Kizco* [1979] Crim.L.R. 465. See also Kenny, *op. cit.*, who, as well as making a number of useful observations on the topic generally, points out that the whole concept of "mental responsibility" introduced for diminished responsibility by statute is an odd one.

NOTE 91. Add: the fact that an expert on glass said that he could not be "sure" that glass found on the accused's shoes came from premises the accused was alleged to have burgled did not mean that the jury were not entitled to be sure of the accused's guilt—see *R.* v. *Penman* (1986) 82 Cr.App.R. 44 (C.A.). (The fact that the expert there expressed himself to be 99 per cent. certain made the case a strong one; but the principle that scientific probability and jury certainty are distinct is of general application.)

27–36 NOTE 14. Add *R.* v.*Grossman and Skirving* [1985] 2 All E.R. 705 (1985) 81 Cr.App.R. 9 (C.A.). In that case, expert evidence as to the nature and effects of cocaine was called by the prosecution on the prosecution under the Obscene Publications Act of the publishers of a book advocating the use of cocaine. It was held that the evidence was admissible because it did not go to the question of whether or not the reader was likely to be depraved or corrupted, but only assisted the jury in understanding what was the effect of cocaine, a matter of which they might be entirely ignorant, and without knowledge of which they would be unable to come to an informed decision.

27–41 to 27–42 The courts are today much less anxious than they were formerly to exclude expert evidence. Many, if not most, of the cases cited in these two paragraphs in which expert evidence was excluded are unlikely to be followed today.

(c) OPINIONS OF NON-EXPERTS

Identity: resemblance: photographs

27–62 NOTE 99a. In committal proceedings, the justices have *no* discretion to exclude dock identifications, because it is their duty to consider all admissible evidence, and the discretion is for the trial judge to exercise; *R.* v. *Horsham Justices, ex p. Bukhari* (1982) 74 Cr.App. 294 (D.C.); *R.* v. *Highbury Corner Magistrates' Court, ex parte Boyce* [1984] Crim.L.R. 294 (D.C.).

NOTE 1. Home Office Circular 109/78 is replaced by the *Code of Practice for the Identification of Persons by Police Officers* under the Police and Criminal Evidence Act, 1984.

Failure to comply with the Code may lead to the court exercising a discretion to exclude the identification, as where a confrontation was unfairly arranged: *R.* v. *Leckie and Enslie* [1983] Crim.L.R. 543. This was a decision on the Circular, but it is submitted that the existence of the discretion has not been affected by the introduction of the Code. By section 67(11) of the Police and Criminal Evidence Act 1984, the Code, if "relevant to any question arising in the proceedings . . . shall be taken into account in determining that question. To what question is compliance with the Code relevant? One question may be the reliability of the identification. Another question is thought to be whether the judge should exercise his discretion to exclude evidence of identification. (It is surely a breach of the Code, or an act which fails to comply with it, which is relevant to these questions; but this objection may be merely pedantic.)

NOTE 4a. Add: *R.* v. *Creamer* (1985) 80 Cr.App.R. 226 (C.A.). An identification was admitted although the witness failed to point out the accused during the parade, but identified him by his (approximate) position immediately after the parade was finished. This was a case under the Circular. Under the Code, Annex A, paragraph 7 provides (as did the Circular) that the whole procedure should take place in the presence of the accused (or his solicitor or friend); but paragraph 16 deals specifically with the situation which arose in *Creamer* (above) and provides that the accused and any representative present must be informed, and "consideration . . . given to allowing the witness a second opportunity to identify the suspect."

NOTE 9. Add: Photographs from foreign criminal records are admissible to identify the accused in extradition proceedings; and there may be proved without a statement from a representative of the relevant Criminal Record Office. The exclusion of such photographs is not discretionary; it can occur only as a result of an exclusionary rule: *re Voets* [1986] Crim.L.R. 465 (D.C.).

27–63 Add at end: evidence of identification from a video-tape of the actual crime is permissible: *R.* v. *Grimer* [1982] Crim.L.R. 674 (C.A.); but where a police officer and a store detective identified the accused from a video-tape of another similar crime committed a week after the one which was the subject of the charge, their evidence of their identification was held inadmissible: *R.* v. *Fowden and White* [1982] Crim.L.R. 588 (C.A.).

Again, film of a robbery actually being committed was admitted to enable the jury to identify the accused: see *R.* v. *Dodson* (1984) 79 Cr.App.R. 220 (C.A.). Such a demonstration is not equivalent to a dock identification. Photographs of the accused taken on other occasions may be used to assist the jury in trying to make their identification. There are no rigid rules governing this novel situation; but a trial judge should warn a jury of the dangers inherent in reliance on photographs: see *ibid.*

27–64 NOTE 19. Add: *R.* v. *Curry and Keeble* [1983] Crim.L.R. 827 (C.A.) follows *R.* v. *Oakwell* (see text).

NOTE 19. Add: In *R.* v. *Clifton* [1986] Crim.L.R. 399 (C.A.) a direction to a jury was criticised for failing to make express the "special need for caution" in identification cases, and for failing to warn the jury specifically that even in cases where a person is alleged to have recognised the accused, the identification may be as unreliable as where a stranger is identified. See also *The Insufficiency of Identification Evidence Based on Personal Impression* J. D. Jackson [1986] Crim.L.R. 203.

NOTE 21. Add: see *R.* v. *Shelton and Carter* [1981] Crim.L.R. 776 (C.A.), where fleeting glances at different times by different policemen were held properly to have been allowed to go to the jury, as their identifications had a cumulative effect.

NOTE 21. Add: *R.* v. *Breslin* (1985) 80 Cr.App.R. 226 (C.A.). The directions and warnings set out in *R.* v. *Weeder* (see text) should always be given and the flexibility retained by the decision in *R.* v. *Keane* (see text) is subordinate to that overriding requirement.

NOTE 21a (add at end): it is undesirable to have a trial within a trial on the issue of the admissibility of identification evidence. The position is not analogous to that which obtains when the admissibility of a confession is challenged, nor is there any burden of proof on the Crown to prove that the identification evidence is admissible. It is simply a matter of weight for the jury. See *R.* v. *Walshe* (1981) 74 Cr.App.R. 85 (C.A.).

Add NOTE 21b. The fact that a store-detective had had a good opportunity for observing an alleged shop-lifter does not exonerate the judge from the duty to warn the jury to approach identification evidence with caution: *R.* v. *Tyson* [1985] Crim.L.R. 48 (C.A.).

Handwriting

27–67 NOTE 34. Add: in *R.* v. *Ewing* [1983] Q.B. 1039 (C.A.) it was held that *R.* v. *Angeli* (see text) was decided *per incuriam*, and that *Blyth* v. *Blyth* [1966] A.C. 643 (H.L.) justified the opposite result, so that in criminal proceedings proof of handwriting under section 8 of the Criminal Procedure Act 1865 must be beyond reasonable doubt.

CHAPTER 28.—JUDGMENTS

2.—JUDGMENTS AS CONCLUSIVE EVIDENCE IN SUBSEQUENT PROCEEDINGS

Effect of judgments for and against a party: conditions: dismissals: acquittals

Add after 28–11.

28–11A The Police and Criminal Evidence Act 1984 contains provisions relating to the proof and effect in criminal cases of previous convictions. Section 73 governs the formal mode of proof. Once a conviction is formally proved, it is, if a subsisting conviction (section 75(4)), admissible in evidence for any relevant purpose (section 74(1)). Proof of such a conviction gives rise to a presumption that the person convicted did in fact commit the offence in question, whether (in the later proceedings) the accused (section 74(3)) or some other person (section 74(2)). The presumption is inapplicable in cases where the previous conviction of the accused is adduced because it has "a tendency to show in the accused a disposition to prove the kind of offence with which he is then charged." The standard or proof required to rebut the presumption is left unspecified, as is the answer to the question whether it is the same in relation to section 74(2) as it is in relation to section 74(3). The presumption does not seem to apply where a conviction is admitted, notwithstanding the similar fact rule, for a purpose other than showing a disposition to a particular crime, for example where it is introduced to show the accused's presume at the scene of the crime (he having been convicted of an offence which took place at the same time as it is alleged in later proceedings a further offence was committed) or to show the accused's disposition to advance a similar alibi defence.

(2) *Merger*

28–24 NOTE 37. Add: *Telfair Shipping* v. *Interseas Carriers* [1982] 2 Lloyd's Rep. 351, where it was held that arbitration awards do not give rise to a merger, but where not all the authorities cited in the text appear to have been brought to the court's attention. The case went off in any event on the application of the rule in *Conquer* v. *Boot* (see text at n. 34).

28–25 NOTE 34. Add: In *The Argo Hellas* [1984] 1 Lloyd's Rep. 296, it was held that an arbitration award in respect of a *debt* did not give rise to a merger in the same way as an award of damages. We share the doubts of Mustill & Boyd, *Commercial Arbitration*, p. 362, as to the validity of the distinction. There may truly be a "distinction between an award which merely establishes and measures a liability under the contract and an award of damages which supersedes the liability under the contract" (see *per* Lord Pearson in *Bloemen Ltd.* v. *Gold Coast City* [1973] A.C. 115 at 126); but that is not the same distinction as the one between awards of debt and of damages, but between a declaration of right and an award which orders one party to pay a sum of money to the other.

NOTE 37. Add: Mustill & Boyd, *op. cit.* p. 361 doubt whether the doctrine of merger applies to arbitration awards, and these doubts have been echoed by Lloyd J. in *Telfair Shipping* v. *Interseas Carriers* [1983] 2 Lloyd's Rep. 351. He nonetheless held, following *Conquer* v. *Boot* (see text), that even in arbitrations all damage arising from one cause of action must be assessed at the same time. The distinction from litigation appears to rest on the rule that in the case of arbitration, there is no rule that all causes of action arising out of one contract must be brought forward at the same time. It is thought that this is *not* the merger rule, but what can be called the "whole case" rule. Merger is merely the procedural consequence of a judgment being given on a particular cause of action. There is another rule that a party to an action is bound to bring forward all causes which might properly be subsumed in that action. This rule does not apply in arbitrations in the same way, partly because of the possibility of serial arbitrations, and partly because of the uncertain scope of the arbitrators' jurisdiction. It is however respectfully submitted that the doctrine of merger *does* have effect in arbitrations, and it is only the terrible confusion which surrounds the terminology of *res judicata* which obscures that fact.

NOTE 43. Even in relation to actions as opposed to arbitrations, the whole case rule (see above) does not apply to wholly separate and distinct causes of action. See *Lawlor* v. *Gray* [1984] 3 All E.R. 345, where the distinction between claims for debt and claims for damages was again the foundation of a decision that there had been no merger. See also *Overstone* v. *Shipway* [1962] 1 W.L.R. 117 (C.A.).

NOTE 41. *The Alletta* (see text) was not followed in Singapore in *the Daien Maru No. 18* [1986] 1 Lloyd's Rep. 387, but we prefer the result in the English case, even if some of the reasoning is open to question.

(3) *Estoppel by Judgment*

28–26 Add at end: *R.* v. *Secretary of State, ex p. Hackney B.C.* [1984] 1 W.L.R. 592 (C.A.). Although applications for judicial review are technically civil proceedings, they do not give rise to an issue estoppel, because there is no true *lis* between the Crown and the Respondent or even between the Applicant and the Respondent, and because the position of the court in such cases is similar to that which it holds in criminal cases, in that it is not simply resolving a dispute between two litigants but discharging a duty to the public in administering public justice. Even if there is room for the doctrine to operate (and it was said to be questionable whether the Crown would ever be bound by the doctrine) it would often be difficult to identify the issue decided by the previous decision. The protection for the Crown and the citizen lies in the ability of the court to put a stop to vexatious proceedings. (There was a fuller discussion of the point in the court below, whose judgments were approved on appeal: see [1983] 1 W.L.R. 524 (D.C.).)

28–36 For a clear statement of the principle that everything which is necessarily decided by a court in the course of reaching its decision can give rise to an issue estoppel, see *Tracomin S.A.* v. *Sudan Oil Seeds* [1983] 1 All E.R. 404 at 413a. *Cf. the Balder London (No. 2)* [1983] 1 Lloyd's Rep. 492.

28–49 NOTE 7. Add: *the Messiniaki Bergen* [1983] 1 All E.R. 382 was a case where the principle of giving effect to a foreign judgment by way of issue estoppel was again affirmed, though Bingham J. proceeded with the caution advocated by the House of Lords (see text, NOTE 6) and refused to give effect to an American decision on the ground that there was conflicting expert evidence on the question of whether or not under U.S. law the decision was final. For the purposes of determining whether or not a foreign decision is final and conclusive on the merits, the principles applicable in cases involving issue estoppel are slightly different from those where the question is whether or not there has been a submission to the jurisdiction of the foreign court, by an argument about the merits: see the *Tracomin* case *supra*.

A decision as to procedure alone is not a decision on the merits; but a decision which finds the facts, decides the law, and applies the latter to the former, is a decision on the merits even if the resultant finding is merely that the foreign court does not have jurisdiction: see *The Sennar* [1985] 2 All E.R. 104 (H.L.).

NOTE 7a. It has been asserted, no doubt correctly, but apparently without argument, that the doctrine of issue estoppel applies to arbitrations: see *Qatar Petroleum* v. *Shell* [1983] 2 Lloyd's Rep. 35 (C.A.); *Northern Regional Health Authority* v. *Derek Crouch Construction Ltd.* [1984] 2 All E.R. 175 (C.A.). The arbitrations in these two cases were English ones. It remains to be seen whether the modern enthusiasm for finality extends to foreign arbitration awards, though it is hard to see that there is any logical justification for excluding them from the scope of issue estoppel.

(4) *Matrimonial Causes*

28–54 Add at end: NOTE 32a. In the same way, where discretionary relief has been sought, circumstances may change, so that the discretion falls to be exercised anew, at least where the relief originally sought was essentially of an interlocutory nature. This seems to be the effect of *Thyssen-Bornemisza* v. *Thyssen-Bornemisza* [1985] 1 All E.R. 328 (C.A.).

(6) *Vexation cases*

28–58 NOTE 83. Add: *Bragg* v. *Oceanus Mutual* [1982] 2 Lloyd's Rep. 132 (C.A.), where the same defendants to two separate actions arising out of the same complex of insurance arrangements were held entitled to amend at a late stage in the second action, having done so also in the first action and lost on all points. *Hunter* v. *Chief Constable* (see text) was distinguished; and the same approach was adopted in *Rayner (J. H.) (Mincing Lane) Ltd.* v. *Bank fur Gemeinwirtschaft A.G.* [1983] 1 Lloyd's Rep. 462 (C.A.).

D. Criminal cases

(a) *Autrefois acquit and autrefois convict*

28–59 NOTE 5. Add: *R.* v. *Hay* (1983) 77 Cr.App.R. 70 (C.A.). The accused signed a confession to both arson and burglary. At his trial for arson, where the confession was tendered in evidence with the parts relating to the alleged burglary blanked out, he alleged that the confession had been fabricated by the police and was acquitted. At his trial on the burglary charge, he introduced the whole of the confession, and sought to adduce evidence of his acquittal on the charge of arson, and to call a witness who would provide him with an alibi for the alleged arson. The trial judge refused to allow him to adduce either type of evidence, and his conviction was quashed, following *Sambasivam*'s case (see text). It was said that once the acquittal was before the jury, it was unnecessary to call the alibi witness, though that would not have been so had the burglary charge been heard before the arson. It would certainly have been extraordinary if the prosecution had been able to treat the confession as severable in such a way as to prevent the accused from attacking its reliability by disproving a material part of it. It is, however, difficult to see how absolute fidelity to the principle of *D.P.P.* v. *Humphrys* (see text § 28–61) (that there is no issue estoppel in criminal cases) was maintained in *R.* v. *Hay*. In *D.P.P.* v. *Humphrys*, it was said that, while the prosecution could not seek to challenge an acquittal in a subsequent prosecution on the same facts, it was open to them to call evidence against the accused on the charge before the court, even though that evidence showed that the accused had in fact been guilty of the offence of which he had previously been acquitted (see text, note 99). On that footing, Hay's acquittal on the previous charge of arson did not have the result that the confession to that offence was automatically and irrebuttably shown to be false thereby. It remained open to the prosecutor to show, directly or indirectly, that the confession was true, and to that extent it is thought that the evidence of the alibi witness *must* have been relevant and admissible notwithstanding the adduction of the acquittal. See also *R.* v. *Doosti* (1985) 82 Cr.App.R. 181 (C.A.) (*infra* § 28–61 n. 61).

NOTE 7. Add: An accused cannot plead *autrefois acquit* where the trial judge has directed a verdict of not guilty to be entered, without the accused having been arraigned, because the judge had no jurisdiction to adopt such a course, and the accused had not yet been put in danger of conviction: *R.* v. *Griffiths* [1981] Crim.L.R. 343 (C.A.). Likewise, an accused who pleaded guilty to an offence before justices, was remanded for social inquiry reports, and committed another offence while on remand, was unable to plead *autrefois convict* when he was committed for trial on *both* charges, because there had never been a "conviction" for the offence for which the social inquiry reports were awaited: *R.* v. *Gordon* [1983] Crim.L.R. 735.

28–60 NOTE 23. Add *cf. R.* v. *Carpenter* [1981] Crim.L.R. 562.

NOTE 23a. Add: In *R.* v. *Thomas* (1984) 79 Cr.App.R. 200 (C.A.) it was held that a person convicted of a crime by a *foreign* court of competent jurisdiction might be able to raise the conviction in bar to a subsequent prosecution in the U.K. for the same offence. In order successfully to plead *autrefois convict* in such a case, however, there must really have been in jeopardy on the occasion of the first trial. The accused cannot therefore rely on such a conviction if he was convicted in absentia, and there was no realistic prospect of punishment by the Court which convicted him.

NOTE 24c. Add: the Court of Appeal has power to order a *venire de novo* only where the irregularity in the previous trial has vitiated utterly the previous hearing: *Rose* v. *D.P.P.* [1982] A.C. 822 (H.L.).

(b) *Double jeopardy*

28–61 NOTE 55; NOTE 60. Add: There are now several examples of cases where the Courts have applied the principle that, independently of the doctrines of *autrefois acquit* and *convict*, prosecutions will not be allowed to proceed if they are oppressive and an abuse of the process of the court. The grounds which have so far been invoked for the exercise of this jurisdiction are that there has been a very long delay in the institution of the prosecution, or that a new prosecution will in effect amount to trying a man for an offence for which he has already stood trial: see *R.* v. *Gray's Justices, ex p. Graham* [1982] 3 W.L.R. 596 (D.C.) (delay); *R.* v. *Lord and Fraser* [1983] Crim.L.R. 191 (delay); *Dewhurst* v. *Foster* [1982] Crim.L.R. 582 (quasi-estoppel); *Smith* v. *Birch and Harrington* [1983] Crim.L.R. 193 (quasi-estoppel).

Lord Salmon in *Humphreys* v. *D.P.P.* (see text) left open the question of whether inferior courts had the power to stay a criminal prosecution on the ground that it was vexatious. A similar reservation was expressed in *R.* v. *Horsham JJ ex p. Reeves* (1980) 73 Cr.App.R. 227 (D.C.). The distinction between inferior and superior courts appears not to have been argued, and the power has been exercised by magistrates' courts on several occasions and upheld by the Divisional Court: *R.* v. *Brentford JJ ex p. Wong* (1981) 73 Cr.App.R. 63 (D.C.); *R.* v. *Oxford JJ ex p. Smith* [1982] R.T.R. 201 (D.C.); *R.* v. *Watford JJ ex p. Outrim* [1982] Crim.L.R. 593 (D.C.); *R.* v. *Derby JJ ex p. Brooks* [1984] Crim.L.R. 754 (D.C.).

This line of cases has been carried to what appear to be rather extreme lengths. The decision in *Humphrys* may no doubt be invoked to prevent repeated prosecutions of the same man for what is substantially if not technically the same offence as one for which he has already stood trial. It has also been prayed in aid in the Crown Court as a means of preventing a prosecution of A going ahead where a prosecution against B arising out of the same facts has failed: *R.* v. *Intervision* [1984] Crim.L.R. 350 (distributor acquitted of offence relating to allegedly obscene publication; prosecution of supplier stayed); *R.* v. *Noe* [1985] Crim.L.R. (for "distributor" read "husband," for "supplier" read "wife"). It is respectfully submitted that *Humphrys* v. *D.P.P.* has not introduced the maxim *nemo debet unius vexari* into English law, and that these prosecutions ought to have been allowed to proceed. It has at any rate been held that the mere fact that evidence in support of a prosecution has been illegally obtained is not a ground for seeking a stay of the prosecution: *R.* v. *Heston-Francois* (1984) 78 Cr.App.R. 209 (C.A.) (distinguishing *R.* v. *Bow St. JJ ex p. Mackeson* (1982) 75 Cr.App.R. 24 (D.C.)).

NOTE 61. Add: Moreover, where an accused was convicted of an offence before justices, and secured an acquittal on appeal by means of perjury, it was held that the appellate decision could be set aside, as having been obtained by fraud, so that the pre-existing conviction was reinstated: *R.* v. *Wolverhampton Crown Court, ex p. Crofts* [1982] 3 All E.R. 702 (D.C.). In *R.* v. *Ireland* [1985] Crim.L.R. 367 (C.A.), a defendant who had been convicted before the Crown Court of driving while disqualified had his conviction set aside when he was later acquitted by justices of various other driving charges arising out of the same incident. It was said that not only the evidence of the additional witnesses but the verdict of the lay bench showed that the conviction was unsafe and unsatisfactory. The accused's own account that he had never been driving at all was countered by police evidence that he had changed places with his wife; so that it would have been particularly unfortunate if he had been wrongly convicted; but it is hard to see why the evidence of new witnesses should not rather have been introduced as part of a general re-assessment of the evidence on appeal (provided that the conditions were satisfied for the admission of fresh evidence on appeal), and still more obscure what relevance could lie in the justices' assessment of the evidence. In effect the second prosecution became a novel remedy, an appeal by way of rehearing from the Crown Court to lay justices. An acquittal on an identical charge is not admissible in chief for the purpose of undermining a second prosecution for committing the same crime (on a different occasion) as was alleged against the accused on the first hearing, even though it was the same police officer whose evidence was the foundation of both charges: *R.* v. *Doosti* (1985) 82 Cr.App.R. 181 (C.A.). (The evidence was admitted in rebuttal: see *supra* § 13–47A.) In that case, it was taken as significant that the previous acquittal was not inconsistent with the reliability of the police officer's evidence. We think that even if it had been a case where the acquittal entailed the rejection of the police officer's evidence, it still could not have been introduced in examination of the accused in chief, but only in cross-examination of the police officer. See also *R.* v. *Hay* (1983) 77 Cr.App.R. 70 (C.A.).

EXAMPLES

28–62 Paragraph (4)—add at end: see *R.* v. *Pervez and Khan* [1983] Crim.L.R. 108 (C.A.). A judge rejected an application to exclude on the ground that they were involuntary, the confessions of two men jointly charged with an offence, and having subsequently acceded to an application that the accused be tried separately, refused to hear fresh applications in relation to the same confessions in the separate trials. His decision was upheld, although it was said that the application for separation of the trials should have been made at the outset. *Quaere* whether the same result would have been permitted if the separate trials had been heard by a different judge.

28–98A The Rule in *Hollington* v. *Hewthorn* has now been abolished for criminal cases also by the Police and Criminal Evidence Act, 1984. Section 74(1) provides that the conviction of a person other than the accused may always be tendered in evidence to prove (where it is relevant to do so) that that third party was guilty of that offence. Section 74(2) in effect creates a persuasive presumption of the conviction, and it is thought, though the statute fails to distinguish the two cases, that the quantum of proof required to displace the presumption will vary according to whether the prosecution or the accused wishes to rely on the third party's conviction. Section 75 provides that the information, complaint, indictment or charge sheet on which the conviction is founded are admissible to prove the facts of the offence. See further *supra* § 28–11A.

CHAPTER 29.—PROBATES ETC.

29–08 NOTE 50. Although the reports of Inspectors appointed by the Department of Trade are not admissible in evidence for the purpose of establishing the facts they contain, they are admissible for the purpose of shewing the Inspectors' opinions, and, if unchallenged, are grounds for obtaining a winding up order: *Savings and Investment Bank* v. *Gasco B.V.* [1984] 1 All E.R. 296; see also *re St. Piran* [1981] 1 W.L.R. 1300.

EXAMPLES

28–102 NOTE 86. A plea of guilty in a criminal trial is an admission like any other, and is admissible in subsequent civil proceedings. It is not, however, a "solemn judicial confession of the fact," and *R.* v. *Fontaine Moreau* (see text) does not hold that it is: see *Cromarty* v. *Monteith* (1957) 8 D.L.R. (2d) 112.

CHAPTER 30.—PROCESS, ETC.

Subpoena duces tecum: judge's order

30–09 Add at end: A *subpoena duces tecum* will not be issued against a foreign bank in respect of documents in another country, notwithstanding what the bank has a branch in this country: *MacKinnon* v. *Donaldson Lufkin* [1986] 2 W.L.R. 453. The Bankers' Books Evidence Act 1879, section 7 and the *subpoena duces tecum* are on the same footing as regards jurisdiction: see *R.* v. *Grossman* (1981) 73 Cr.App.R. 302 (C.A.) (although in that case the court did not have jurisdiction, but proceeded *per incuriam*).

Commissions

30–30 Where it appears that a witness will be unavailable to give evidence at the trial, the court may order that his or her evidence be taken on commission. The procedure is governed by R.S.C. Ord. 39. It may be invoked where the witness is ill, infirm, expected to die or is expected to go abroad. It may also be employed where a witness is already abroad. The evidence is usually taken before an examiner, who will note rather than rule on objections to the admissibility of evidence. There is power for the examination to be conducted before a judge, but this is not very often used.

30–31 Where a witness is out of the jurisdiction and his voluntary attendance cannot be secured, Letters of Request may be issued invoking the assistance of the foreign court having jurisdiction over him. See Supreme Court Act 1980, section 36 and R.S.C. Order 39 rr. 2–3. Some countries will assist as a matter of international convention, either because they are party to a bilateral treaty with the U.K. or because they are party to the Hague Convention on Taking Evidence Abroad in Civil or Commercial Matters (1970); some countries will assist as a matter of comity; and some countries will not assist at all. The status of various countries is set out in the Supreme Court Practice 1985 39/2–3/2 to 39/2–3/6. Letters of Request will not be issued to a foreign court where the purpose of obtaining the evidence is to prove that the government of the country to whose courts the Letters are addressed was a participant in a fraud: *Setebello Ltd.* v. *Banco Totta* [1985] 1 W.L.R. 1050 (C.A.).

30–32 The converse case, that of evidence being taken in England for the purposes of some foreign proceedings, is governed by the Evidence (Proceedings in Other Jurisdictions) Act 1975 and by R.S.C. Order 70. An important examination of some of the basic principles is to be found in *re Anders Jahre* [1986] 1 Lloyd's Rep. 496 (C.A.).

CHAPTER 31.—COMPETENCY AND COMPELLABILITY, OATH AND AFFIRMATION

1.—COMPETENCY

History of the Law

Former disqualifications: interest (parties, consorts, other witnesses), atheism, crime

31–06 *Husband and wife.* See now Police and Criminal Evidence Act 1984, section 80.

Present Law—General Rule

(a) Incompetency from defective intellect

31–08 Where the judge concludes after inquiry that a witness is competent in the sense that he understands the nature of the proceedings, but is not aware of the divine sanction of the oath, the witness should nevertheless be sworn unless he objects (in which case he may affirm): *R.* v. *Bellamy* [1986] Crim.L.R. 54.

(b) Incompetency from infancy

31–09 For judicial comment on the use in evidence of video recordings of interviews with very young children and on the value of such interviews and interviewing techniques, for the purposes of wardship proceedings, see *In re E (A minor), The Times*, September 16, 1986.

Incompetency or competency peculiar to criminal proceedings

1. Witnesses who need not swear or affirm

31–11 *Children.* The Court of Appeal re-affirmed in *R.* v. *Campbell* [1983] Crim.L.R. 174, that the two principles to be followed when considering whether a child should properly be sworn were set out in *Hayes* [1977] 1 W.L.R. 234 (quoted in the text).

2. Witnesses for the prosecution

31–12 (1) *Accused or spouse.* A spouse is now in all criminal proceedings a competent witness for the prosecution: Police and Criminal Evidence Act 1984, section 80(1)(*a*). There is one exception to this general rule. If a husband and wife are jointly charged, neither spouse is competent to give evidence for the prosecution unless that spouse is not liable to be convicted of the offence, or no longer so liable: see section 80(4). Section 80 is set out in the Appendix to this Supplement.

NOTE 60. The Evidence Act 1877 was repealed by the Statute Law (Repeals) Act 1981 s.1(1) Schedule 1, Part 1.

31–13 Effect of judicial separation, etc. Section 80(5) of the 1984 Act renders a former spouse competent (and compellable) to give evidence as if that person and the defendant had never been married. Section 1(*d*) of the Criminal Evidence Act 1898 is repealed.

It continues to be the law that a bigamous marriage is no marriage for the purposes of competence. The wife of a second polygamous marriage is not regarded as married for these purposes: *R.* v. *Khan (Junaid), The Times*, June 10, 1986 (C.A.).

3. Witnesses for the defence

31–16 (1) *The Accused.* The wife or husband of the accused remains competent to give evidence for the defence, but the statutory provision is now section 80(1)(*b*) of the Police and Criminal Evidence Act 1984.

31–17 (2) *Comment by counsel.* Section 1(*b*) of the Criminal Evidence Act 1898 is replaced, in relation to a wife or husband of the accused, by section 80(8) of the 1984 Act. See also *R.* v. *Naudeer* [1984] 3 All E.R. 1036; 80 Cr.App.R. 9.

31–20 Sections 1(*c*) and 4 of the Criminal Evidence Act 1898 have been repealed by the 1984 Act: Schedule 7, Part V. A spouse is now usually a competent witness for the prosecution: section 80(1)(*a*), (4); see *ante*, § 31–12.

31–21 Section 30(3) of the Theft Act 1968 is repealed by the 1984 Act: Schedule 7, Part V.

31–22 The spouse of the accused is now compellable to give evidence for the prosecution or for a person jointly charged with the accused only if the offence is one of violence to that spouse, violence to a person under 16 or a sexual offence in respect of a person under 16: see the precise definition of such offences in the Police and Criminal Evidence Act 1984, section 80(3). However, if a husband and wife are jointly charged, neither spouse is so compellable unless that spouse is not liable to be convicted of the offence, or no longer so liable: see section 80(4).

In *R.* v. *Pitt* [1983] Q.B. 25; 75 Cr.App.R. 254, (C.A.), it was held:

1. A wife retains the right of refusal to give evidence against her husband up to the point when, with full knowledge of that right, she takes the oath in the witness box;
2. If she waives her right of refusal, she becomes an ordinary witness;
3. She may therefore, if appropriate, be treated as hostile.

The Court said that a judge should explain to the wife, in the absence of the jury, before she takes the oath, that she has the right to refuse to give evidence, but that if she chooses to give evidence, she may be treated like any other witness.

Summary

31–23 to 31–25 As to the competence and compellability of the spouse of the accused, see now Police and Criminal Evidence Act 1984, section 80.

Objections: How Taken

31–28 NOTE 29. The correct reference to *R.* v. *Khan* should be (1981) 73 Cr.App.R. 190; [1981] Crim.L.R. 330.

2.—COMPELLABILITY

31–30 (1) As to the compellability of the spouse of an accused person, see now Police and Criminal Evidence Act 1984, section 80.

31–31 Companies Act 1948, section 167(3) has been replaced by Companies Act 1985, section 436.

3.—Oath and Affirmation

31–32 It appears that even if it appears that a witness is not aware of the divine sanction of the oath, he should be sworn unless he objects (in which case he may affirm): *R.* v. *Bellamy, ante*, § 31–08.

CHAPTER 32.—CORROBORATION

General principles

32–01 Note 6. In *R.* v. *Donat* (1986) Cr.App.R. 173, the Court of Appeal held that the failure by the trial judge to direct the jury that the corroborative evidence must implicate the accused was corrected by the judge's putting forward of a number of potentially corroborative pieces of evidence which did implicate the accused. Moreover the second limb of the principle in *Baskerville* (see text) is now qualified in the case of aiders and abettors. In *R.* v. *Olaleye* (1986) 82 Cr.App.R. 337, it was held that "It would be absurd in regard to an aider and abettor . . . to reapply the corroboration rule to a complainant's evidence affecting him, to establish the already proven, namely, that she was a reliable and truthful witness." Absurd as it may be, that process would have seemed to be required by *Baskerville*.

Requirements as to corroboration in certain circumstances

Statutory provisions

32–03 (1) *Perjury*. Corroboration as to the falsity of the statement is not required (a) in those rare cases in which the prosecution does not seek to prove the falsity of the statement and (b) where the defendant admitted that the statement was untrue: *R.* v. *Rider, The Times*, April 30, 1986 (C.A.).

(7) *Road Traffic Regulation Act 1967*

32–04 The Divisional Court held that justices were wrong in law in deciding that the evidence provided by a "Muniquip" speed meter, although in principle capable of providing corroboration, had not been of sufficient quality to do so. The justices were wrong because there was no evidence to contradict the evidence of the speed meter: *Burton* v. *Gilbert* [1984] R.T.R. 162. See also *Collinson* v. *Mabbott, The Times*, October 10, 1984. The 1967 Act has been consolidated in the Road Traffic Regulation Act 1984.

Rules of Practice

(2) *Accomplices*

32–06
1. The judge is not obliged to give a full accomplice warning unless the witness was involved in the crime charged.
2. If there is material to suggest that the witness may have a purpose of his own to serve in giving evidence the judge should warn the jury to proceed with caution. The appropriate warning is a matter for the judge. *R.* v. *Beck* [1982] 1 W.L.R. 461; 74 Cr.App.R. 221; *R.* v. *Stainton* [1983] Crim.L.R. 171; *R.* v. *King, The Times*, January 13, 1983.

The Court of Appeal in the above cases was considering whether the full accomplice warning was necessary in cases where the witness might be thought to have an interest of his own to serve. In *Beck*, *supra*, the witnesses had an alleged purpose in giving evidence, namely to cover up false representations made in an insurance claim. The insurance claim was not connected with the offence charged against the defendant. It was argued that these witnesses had a "substantial interest of their own to serve and a full accomplice direction should be given." The court rejected this argument. Ackner L.J., giving the judgment of the court, said: "While we in no way wish to detract from the obligation upon a judge to advise a jury to proceed with caution where there is material to suggest that a witness's evidence may be tainted by an improper motive, and the strength of that advice must vary according to the facts of the case, we cannot accept that there is any obligation to give the accomplice warning with all that entails, when it is common ground that there is no basis for suggesting that the witness is a participant in any way involved in the crime the subject matter of the trial" (74 Cr.App.R. 221, 228). The court was of the view that if and insofar as *Prater* [1960] 2 Q.B. 464 was not a decision on its own facts it did not extend the law in *Davies* [1954] A.C. 378. The court also said that the phrase (in the judgment of the court in *Prater* at p. 466) "it is desirable that in cases where a person may be regarded as having some purpose of his own to serve, the warning against uncorroborated evidence should be given" is related to cases where witnesses may be participants or involved in the crime charge (p. 227). In *R.* v. *Stainton, supra*, the defendant was charged with theft. A stolen cheque with a forged endorsement had been processed through the building society account of C. At the defendant's trial C. gave evidence that the defendant asked him to process the cheque. C. denied that he had been involved in the theft or the forgery. The recorder told the jury that C. was not an accomplice but that he might have some axe to grind and they should be careful about accepting his evidence. The defendant appealed against his subsequent conviction on the ground that the full accomplice warning should be given. The Court of Appeal dismissed the appeal, applying *Beck* and holding that there was no evidence on which the recorder could have left to the jury the question of whether C. was an accomplice or not. The court said that where a judge merely concluded that the witness might have some purpose of his own to serve in giving evidence, then the warning he gave was a matter for him and that part of the judgment in *R.* v. *Jenkins* (1981) 72 Cr.App.R. 354 which had suggested that in those circumstances the full accomplice warning was necessary was no longer correct following the decision in *Beck*.

(c) *Co-defendants*

32–09 1. When the defendant gives evidence against a co-defendant the judge is not obliged to give the full accomplice warning: *R.* v. *Loveridge and Loveridge* (1982) 76 Cr.App.R. 125;

2. It is a matter for the discretion of the judge to decide on an appropriate warning when co-defendants give evidence against each other. He should at least warn the jury to examine the evidence of each with care because each has or may have an interest of his own to serve. This warning should suffice to ensure that the jury regards the evidence with proper caution. Whether the judge should advise the jury to look for corroboration and whether he should specify what evidence may be corroboration is a matter for the judge, having regard to the nature and severity of the attack made by one co-defendant on another. The content of the warning or advice is best formulated by the trial judge. *R.* v. *Knowlden and Knowlden* (1983) 77 Cr.App.R. 94.

The Court of Appeal quashed a conviction where the judge failed to direct the jury on the dangers of relying on accomplice evidence and failed to warn the jury of the need to approach with caution the evidence of co-defendants who each blamed the other for offences: *R.* v. *Mainwaring and Madders* (1982) 74 Cr.App.R. 99. The court said (at p. 105) that it was just the sort of case in which the judge should have warned the jury to approach the evidence of co-defendants, so far as one inculpated the other, with considerable caution.

(4) *Sexual offences*

32–12 NOTE 73. Add: Where, on a rape charge, consent was in issue, medical evidence capable of showing that a buggery on the same occasion was forcible was capable of corroborating the victim's assertion that intercourse was also forcible: *R.* v. *Jarrett* [1985] Crim.L.R. 306. There is no requirement for a corroboration warning to be given on a charge under section 31 of the 1956 Act, exercising control over a prostitute: *R.* v. *Hanton, The Times*, February 14, 1985. In *R.* v. *Birchall and others* (1985) Cr.App.R. 208, the Court of Appeal allowed the appeal and declined to apply the proviso where there was no direction on the corroboration of a complainant even where minimal reliance was placed on her evidence by the prosecution.

(6) *Other "suspect" witnesses*

32–14 The House of Lords has now authoritatively considered this situation in *R.* v. *Spencer and others* [1986] 2 All E.R. 929, a case involving evidence by patients at a special hospital. Where the evidence for the Crown consists solely of the evidence of a witness who is not within one of the accepted classes of suspect witnesses but who, by reason of his particular mental condition and criminal connection, fulfilled analogous criteria, the trial judge is required to warn the jury that it would be dangerous to convict on that witness's uncorroborated evidence. The use of the word "dangerous" is not essential to an adequate warning, provided the jury are made fully aware of the dangers of convicting on such evidence. The House of Lords further held that *R.* v. *Beck* [1982] 1 W.L.R. 461 was rightly decided and that in a case which does not fall into the three established categories and where there exists potential corroborative material the extent to which the trial judge should make reference to that material depends on the facts of each case.

In *R.* v. *Wilkins* [1985] Crim.L.R. 222 (C.A.), it was held that a witness who testifies reluctantly, having been remanded in custody and fined for contempt, is in no special category and her evidence does not attract the necessity for a warning. It is submitted that this decision would be the same after *Spencer and others* (*supra*).

(7) *R.* v. *Turnbull*

32–15 See *R.* v. *Tyson* [1985] Crim.L.R. 48, where the court held that it was "unfortunate" that parts of the *Turnbull* judgment had been paraphrased and elided in the trial judge's summing up. The appeal was, however, dismissed.

Sources of Corroboration

32–17 (10) NOTE 14. Add *R.* v. *Vincent and Taylor* (1983) Crim.L.R. 173 (C.A.)

(11) There was no requirement that corroborative evidence had to relate to the particular incident spoken to by the accomplice: *R.* v. *Beck* (1982) 1 W.L.R. 461; 74 Cr.App.R. 221 approving the dictum of Maule J. in *Mullins* (1848) 3 Cox 531.

NOTE 16. Add: *R.* v. *Timmins* (1981) Crim.L.R. 774; see also *R.* v. *Campbell* (1983) Crim.L.R. 174 as an example of misdirection that certain evidence confirmed that the defendant had committed the offence.

NOTE 17. Add: *R.* v. *Cullinane* [1984] Crim.L.R. 420 where, however, the proviso was applied.

Facts admissible in corroboration

32–18 NOTE 21. Add *R.* v. *Holland and Smith* (1983) Crim.L.R. 545.

A refusal, without good cause, to consent to the taking of an "intimate sample" may be treated as, or as capable of amounting to, corroboration: Police and Criminal Evidence Act 1984, section 62(10).

Lies told by the defendant

32–19 In *R.* v. *Dowley* [1983] Crim.L.R. 168 the Court of Appeal quashed a conviction where corroboration was to be found in lies told by the defendant to the police, but the judge failed to draw the jury's attention to the question whether there might not be some other reason for the defendant's lies than the risk that he might be held guilty of the offence.

R. v. *Lucas* (see text) was applied in *R.* v. *West* (1984) 79 Cr.App.R. 45. The Court of Appeal quashed a conviction where, on a trial for rape and assault, the trial judge had failed to draw the jury's attention to the distinction between the defendant trying to lie himself out of the assault charge and his trying to lie himself out of the rape charge. A lie can only amount to corroboration if it constitutes an attempt by the defendant to lie his way out of conviction on the particular charge in question.

EXAMPLES

32–23 **Affiliation.** Evidence of a blood test report is capable of being "other evidence" corroborating the mother's evidence: *Turner* v. *Blunden* [1986] 2 All E.R. 75.

CHAPTER 33.—RULES OF EVIDENCE RELATING TO THE COURSE OF A TRIAL

1.—PRELIMINARIES

1. Proceedings in open court

33–01 The Report of the Fraud Trials Committee (Chairman, Lord Roskill), 1986, has recommended reforms to the rules of evidence in fraud trials. See particularly chapter 5 of the report.

Justices were held to have been in breach of their duty to hear the whole case in open court in the following circumstances. The defendant appeared before them for offences of driving with defective tyres. During the trial the justices called for a tyre gauge. When they retired they took the tyre gauge with them although no evidence had been given as to how the gauge operated: *R.* v. *Tiverton Justices ex p. Smith* [1980] R.T.R. 280 (D.C.).

33–02 *Exceptions*: The Divisional Court commented recently that it was wholly exceptional and a course of last resort to hear matters in camera. The course was only to be adopted if proceedings in open court would frustrate the process of justice: *R.* v. *Reigate Justices ex p. Argus Newspapers Ltd.* [(1983) 5 Cr.App.R.(S) 181 (D.C.). In that case the Divisional Court criticised justices who heard mitigation in camera in the case of a "supergrass" who had changed his identity and then offended again. The court said that the justices should have applied their minds to other courses which were open to them and which would have been preferable to a hearing in camera.

NOTE 21a. *R.* v. *Ealing Justices ex p. Weafer* is now reported at 74 Cr.App.R. 204.

5. Absence of accused and other parties to proceedings

33–06 The judge's discretion to allow a trial to proceed in the absence of the accused is not limited to cases in which the accused had abused his right to be present or had consented to the trial continuing in his absence. In an appropriate case the judge has a discretion to continue a trial if one of the accused is absent through illness. This discretion should be sparingly used and never if the accused's defence could be prejudiced by his absence: *R.* v. *Howson* (1981) 74 Cr.App.R. 172. See also *R.* v. *O'Nione* [1986] Crim.L.R. 342 (C.A.).

An appellant from the magistrates' court to the Crown Court, if represented by counsel, is not under an obligation to attend personally: *R.* v. *Croydon Crown Court* [1986] 1 W.L.R. 746 (D.C.).

6. Order of witnesses

33–07 In a case in the Crown Court (*R.* v. *Haslam and Wilson* (1983) Crim.L.R. 566 (Bristol Crown Court: Judge Sir Ian Lewis)) it was held that the judge had a discretion to allow the defendant second on the indictment to give evidence first on proper grounds being advanced.

The time for taking the accused's evidence in criminal proceedings is now governed by section 79 of the Police and Criminal Evidence Act 1984 (see Appendix to this supplement). The section states that the accused must be called as the first defence witness unless the court in its discretion otherwise directs.

Obligation to call witnesses

33–08 In *R.* v. *Gallagher* [1983] Crim.L.R. 335, two victims of muggings were examined by a doctor who made a statement about their injuries and was a witness for the prosecution (the report is silent as to whether he was fully or conditionally bound). At the trial the doctor refused to appear. The defendants applied to have the case adjourned so that the doctor might appear. They refused to say why they wanted him to appear. The judge ordered the trial to proceed. The Court of Appeal held that there had been no irregularity since there was no injustice to the defendants in that the discrepancies between the doctor's statement and the complainants' evidence were put fairly before the jury.

Information the prosecution should make available to the defence

(3) *The bad character of the witness*

33–12 In *R.* v. *Paraskeva* (1982) 76 Cr.App.R. 162 the Court of Appeal held that the prosecution's failure to reveal to the defence a conviction of dishonesty was a material irregularity. The defendant was charged with assaulting a health inspector, occasioning him actual bodily harm. The health inspector was the sole prosecution witness. He had come to the defendant's premises in connection with some work which the local council required to be done. He gave evidence that the defendant had assaulted him. The defendant and his father gave evidence that no assault had occurred. There was a "head on collision" of evidence between the two sides according to the Court of Appeal. The health inspector had a conviction for theft seven years before. The prosecution by error did not reveal the conviction to the defence. On appeal the prosecution did not dispute that they were under a duty to reveal the conviction but submitted that the judge would not have permitted the conviction to be put to the witness because it was spent. The Court of Appeal did not accept the submission since it was relevant in a case of this sort for the jury to be told that the prosecution witness had been dishonest in the past.

8. Notice of Alibi: Criminal Justice Act 1967, s.11

33–16 In *R.* v. *Rossborough* (1985) 81 Cr.App.R. 139, the Court of Appeal doubted the validity of the argument in *R.* v. *Watts* as to the relevance of a possible submission of no case (see text), and held that only in rare cases would it be wrong for the alibi notice to be put in.

10. Prosecution's duty to call the evidence it intends to rely upon before the close of its case: omission to call technical evidence

33–26 NOTE 33. Add: *R.* v. *West London Stipendiary Magistrates ex p. Kaminski* [1983] Crim.L.R. 40 may be contrasted with *R.* v. *Gainsborough Justices ex p. Green* [1983] Crim.L.R. 627 as illustrations of the workings of the rule. The former case concerned committal proceedings in which statements were read under section 102 of the Magistrates' Court Act 1980. The defendant made a submission of no case. Before the magistrate ruled on the submission the prosecutor applied for and was granted an adjournment to adduce further evidence. The defendant applied for an order prohibiting the magistrate from hearing further evidence. The Divisional Court refused the application and held, following *Prescott-Clark*, that if at a summary trial magistrates had jurisdiction to allow the prosecution an adjournment to make good a technical *lacuna* in their case then they had equally the jurisdiction to allow an adjournment for the purpose of clarifying an ambiguity in committal proceedings.

In the *Gainsborough Justices* case, on the other hand, the defendant appeared before the justices on summonses laid by a probation officer alleging breaches of a community service order. The probation officer only relied on one breach of the order. The defendant had a good reason for not attending on that occasion. The defendant made a submission of no case. The justices allowed the probation officer to re-open her case and call further evidence of other breaches of the order. The defendant was convicted. He applied to have the justices' decision quashed. The Divisional Court allowed the application and quashed the conviction. Unless there were exceptional circumstances, *e.g.* a purely technical matter which was not in dispute, the court should not allow the prosecution to re-open its case and have a second bite at the cherry.

2.—THE RIGHT TO BEGIN. ORDER OF SPEECHES

The right to begin

33–29 *Criminal cases.* A trial "begins" when a jury is sworn and is seised of the issue: *R.* v. *Tonner and Evans* [1985] 1 All E.R. 807.

3.—EXAMINATION IN CHIEF

Matters Arising During Examination in Chief

(1) Refreshing memory

33–37 It is proper for the judge to suggest that a witness refresh his memory from a document, but generally it is better that a witness remain in court to do so: *R.* v. *Tyagi, The Times*, July 21, 1986 (C.A.).

See Heaton-Armstrong, Police Officers' Notebooks [1985] Crim.L.R. 781.

(6) *Production: inspection: cross-examination*

33–42 The rule in respect of the refreshing of memory, namely that a defendant is entitled to see memory refreshing documents and to cross-examine upon them, should be the same if memory had been refreshed outside the door of the court as if memory was refreshed in the witness box. Counsel for the defence is therefore entitled to see a note book used by a police officer to refresh his memory before going into the witness box (but not in the box) and to cross-examine upon the relevant matters contained within. *Owen* v. *Edwards*, (1984) 77 Cr.App.R. 191 (D.C.).

Police forces increasingly use the practice of making contemporaneous notes of interviews with defendants. Courts then have to decide whether the notes should be exhibited. As a general rule, juries should not be given copies of such notes unless the notes have been:

(a) signed or initialled by the defendant; or
(b) otherwise adopted by him (for which purpose it may be enough if it can be clearly shown that the notes were read over to him and he said they were correct); or
(c) it is necessary for the jury to see the note itself to determine an issue in the case (for instance as to whether they were genuine or not):

R. v. *Fenlon* (1980) 71 Cr.App.R. 307, 310–312; *R*. v. *Dillon*, [1984] Crim.L.R. 100 (C.A.).

In *R*. v. *Marin (John), The Times*, July 1, 1983 the Court of Appeal held that contemporary notes of an interview should not have been exhibited where the defendant had remained silent or answered "no" to questions, only four of which were relevant.

(2) Discrediting or contradicting party's own witness

When the witness is adverse, i.e. hostile

33–45 A wife who chooses to give evidence against her husband may be treated as hostile, but before she gives evidence the judge should explain to her in the absence of the jury that she has the right to refuse to give evidence, but if she does, she can be treated like any other witness: *R*. v. *Pitt* [1983] Q.B. 25; 75 Cr.App.R. 254.

See Newark, The Hostile Witness and the Adversary System [1986] Crim.L.R. 441.

An application to treat a witness as hostile may be made at any time during that witness's evidence, even during re-examination: *R*. v. *Powell* [1985] Crim.L.R. 592 (C.A.). As to re-examination of a hostile witness, see *R*. v. *Wong* [1986] Crim.L.R. 683.

For the procedure where a hostile witness denies that he made parts of a statement, see *R*. v. *Baldwin* [1986] Crim.L.R. 681 (C.A.).

Evidential Value of Testimony and Statement where earlier Inconsistent Statement Proved

33–47 (i) *Criminal proceedings.* In *R*. v. *Thomas* [1985] Crim.L.R. 445, the Court of Appeal held that a judge misdirected a jury in telling them to disregard the evidence of a defence witness who was treated as hostile and who gave some evidence, albeit reluctantly, which supported the defence case.

(3) Previous consistent statements

Previous statements by accused persons

33–56 *R.* v. *Pearce* (see text) was applied in *R.* v. *Kurshid* [1984] Crim.L.R. 288 (C.A.), where a defendant wished to call his solicitor to give evidence that, shortly before making a confession to the police, the defendant had told his solicitor he would make a false confession in order to be released earlier. The Court of Appeal, dismissing his appeal against conviction, held that the case fell squarely within the principle in *R.* v. *Pearce* set out in the text as **Clause (1)**.

33–60 *R.* v. *Duncan (Findlay)* (1981) 73 Cr.App.R. 359 (see text) was followed in *R.* v. *Hamand* (1986) Cr.App.R. 65.

4.—Cross-Examination

(1) Liability to cross-examination

33–64 As to cross-examination on affidavits, see *CBS United Kingdom* v. *Perry* [1985] F.S.R. 421 (Falconer J.) and *E.I. Du Pont* v. *Enka AG, The Times*, July 22, 1986 (C.A.).

(3) Cross-examination as to documents

Execution and contents

33–73 Note 46. See also *R.* v. *Cooper (Warwick)* (1985) 82 Cr.App.R. 74 (C.A.).

(4) Credit

No contradiction on collateral matters: four exceptions

33–87 (4) *Medical evidence affecting reliability of witness's evidence.* See Pattenden, Conflicting Approaches to Psychiatric Evidence in Criminal Trials: England, Canada and Australia [1986] Crim.L.R. 92.

5.—Re-Examination

33–91 In *R.* v. *Harman* [1985] Crim.L.R. 326 (C.A.), it was held that, while in re-examination counsel may invite a witness to refresh his memory from a suitably contemporaneous document, he may not then go on effectively to cross-examine his own witness as to which of two versions given is likely to be more reliable.

6.—Evidence in Rebuttal

Criminal proceedings

33–94 The Court of Appeal has again considered the expression "*ex improviso*" in two reported cases: *R.* v. *Scott* (1984) 79 Cr.App.R. 49 and *R.* v. *Harrington* (1984) 6 Cr.App.R.(S) 182, and has reiterated that the proper test is whether the prosecution could reasonably have foreseen that the particular piece of evidence was necessary to prove the case; it is a matter for the discretion of the trial judge whether that test is satisfied. The prosecution are expected to react reasonably to pre-trial warnings of matters likely to be raised; but not to take notice of "fanciful and unreal statements," even in the form of a letter from the defendant to the D.P.P. before trial: *R.* v. *Hutchinson* (1985) 82 Cr.App.R. 51.

7.—Examination by Judge and Jury Recalling Witness

33–95 In considering whether a conviction has been rendered unsafe by reason of the prejudicial effect of the interruptions of the judge, the Court of Appeal said that the crucial aspect was not the number of interventions but their quality and their effect on the deployment of the defence case and in relation to the judge's attitude as observed by the jury: *R.* v. *Matthews and Matthews* (1984) 78 Cr.App.R. 23.

Note 94. Add: see *R.* v. *McDowell* [1984] Crim.L.R. 486 for a case where the conviction was quashed because of the judge's irregularity in calling a witness to answer a question raised by the jury; and *R.* v. *Roberts* (1985) Cr.App.R. 89 where the Court emphasised that refusing to call a witness himself when requested to do so by counsel was a matter within the trial judge's discretion.

8.—Anticipating and Interposing Evidence: No Evidence to be Called after the Enclosure of the Jury

33–97 The principles stated in *Webb* v. *Leadbetter* do not apply to magistrates exercising their domestic jurisdiction: *R.* v. *Leeds Justices ex p. T.* (1984) 14 Fam.-Law 20. Sheldon J. said that in his opinion it would be difficult to consider any circumstances in which it would be proper before final determination for justices to refuse to hear evidence of potential relevance to the welfare of a child.

In a civil case it has been held that the court has a discretion to admit evidence during the course of counsel's final speeches, to be exercised in the interests of justice. The discretion was not confined to cases where one of the parties had been taken by surprise or misled: *Neigut* v. *Hanama, The Times*, June 6, 1983 (Stuart Smith J).

9.—Statements Made from the Dock

33–98 The right to make an unsworn statement from the dock was abolished by section 72 of the Criminal Justice Act 1982.

10.—Communications between Judge and Jury

33–100 Note 42. Add: *R.* v. *Gibson* (1983) 77 Cr.App.R. 151; *R.* v. *Rafique* [1973] Crim.L.R. 777.

Note 44. The Court of Appeal has emphasised the necessity of disclosing to counsel notes sent by the jury [1985] Crim.L.R. 160.

11.—Evidence after Verdict: Antecedents

33–101 Note 55. Add: It is proper for the judge to hear evidence in cases where there is a difference as to the facts between prosecution and defence in order to ascertain what had taken place in the commission of the crime: *R.* v. *Milligan* (1982) 4 Cr.App.R.(S) 2. If there is a conflict as to the facts between prosecution and defence, it may be resolved in one of two ways:

(i) It may be resolved in an appropriate case by the jury, *e.g.* in cases of wounding or causing grievous bodily harm the issue whether the defendant had the necessary intent under section 18 may be tried by a jury.

(ii) The judge may hear evidence to decide the issue himself. Thus if the issue in a case of buggery with a woman (as in *R.* v. *Newton* (1982) 77 Cr.App.R. 13) is whether the woman consented or not, it is not a matter which can be tried by a jury. In these circumstances the judge may hear evidence to determine the issue. A further example occurs in cases where the defendant puts forward an account as to how the offences occurred which the prosecution does not accept. If it is a matter of little or no importance the judge will not be deterred from passing sentence. There are cases however where the matter raised is so important that the judge may wish to hear evidence in order to determine the issue. Thus, if a defendant admits stealing sums of money but says that the only reason he did so was to pay a ransom for his child who had been kidnapped, the court would be inclined to take a more lenient view of his case than it would otherwise have done. However, if the prosecution says that (on the evidence available) there is not a word of truth in the defendant's account, a sharp conflict arises. The judge may in these circumstances hear evidence to determine the truth.

(iii) If the judge does not hear evidence he must accept the defendant's version as far as possible. (*R.* v. *Newton* (1982) 77 Cr.App.R. 13, 15).

(iv) If the judge does hear evidence, he must direct himself that he must accept the defendant's account unless he is sure that it is untrue (*Ahmed* (1985) 80 Cr.App.R. 295).

33–102 NOTE 56. Add: It is a basic principle of sentencing that the defendant should be sentenced on the basis of the plea tendered and accepted rather than a more serious crime. Thus where a defendant was indicted for (a) attempted arson with intent to endanger life, or being reckless thereto and (b) with attempting arson with intent to damage property, and pleaded guilty to the lesser offence, the Court of Appeal reduced a sentence apparently passed on the basis that he had been reckless as to whether life was endangered: *R.* v. *Booker* (1982) Crim.L.R. 378.

CHAPTER 34.—EVIDENCE TAKEN BEFORE, OR AFTER TRIAL

1.—CIVIL CASES

34–02 While affidavits may contain hearsay, the affidavit should make clear what material was based on information and belief, and indicate the source: *Re N, The Times*, June 19 and 20, 1986 (Lincoln J.).

R.S.C. Order 41, Rule 1(5) as to the form of affidavits has been amended: R.S.C. (Amendment) 1984.

Deposition before examiners

34–07 In the great majority of cases under Ord. 39, r. 1 an examiner will suffice for the examination, save where the greater authority of the judge is required or where the witness is known to be recalcitrant or unruly: In *Re Brickman's Settlements: Brickman* v. *Goddard Trustees (Jersey)* [1982] 1 All E.R. 336, Megarry V.-C.

Further evidence on appeal

34–13 In *K/S A/S Oil Transport* v. *Saudi Research and Development Limited, The Times*, October 28, 1983 it was submitted on behalf of the appellant defendants that special grounds existed for hearing further evidence, namely:

(i) the large sum of money for which judgment was given;
(ii) there was a foreign element in the case;
(iii) negotiations between the parties were taking place up to the date of the hearing.

The Court of Appeal however dismissed the appeal and commented that

(i) the sum involved could not serve to lower the standard of diligence required of the defendants;
(ii) in many modern cases a foreign element was present;
(iii) the negotiations showed that the possibility of a settlement was far from real.

2.—Criminal Cases

(a) Depositions before magistrates or statements tendered under s.102 of the Magistrates' Courts Act 1980

34–21 See *R.* v. *Blithing* (1983) 77 Cr.App.R. 86; § **18–06** *supra* in this supplement. In that case the dead witness had been fully bound.

(c) Depositions taken abroad, and under the Merchant Shipping, Extradition or Fugitive Offenders Acts ■

34–32 Note 49. See *Rees* v. *Home Secretary* [1986] 2 All E.R. 321 (H.L.).

Evidence after trial on appeal

34–36 *R.* v. *Dallas* (see text) was followed in *R.* v. *Lee* [1984] 1 W.L.R. 578. In the same case the Court of Appeal expressed the view that occasions on which it would allow evidence to be called on an appeal against conviction after an unequivocal plea of guilty would be very rare.

34–37 Add at end of second paragraph: and in *R.* v. *Frankum* (1983) 5 Cr.App.R.(S) 259 similarly received evidence from an expert who had *not* testified at trial, where the appeal was against sentence based upon a special verdict.

Note 67. Delete [1978] 1 W.L.R. 735. Insert *The Times*, June 9, 1978.

CHAPTER 36.—CONTENTS OF DOCUMENTS GENERALLY

4.—Judicial Documents

Criminal proceedings

36–56 Notes 53–57. The proof of previous convictions and acquittals of the accused is now largely governed by the Police and Criminal Evidence Act 1984, section 73. The relevant parts of section 13 of the Evidence Act 1851, section 6 of the Criminal Procedure Act 1865 and section 18 of the Prevention of Crime Act 1871 are repealed by Sched. VII of the 1984 Act. For trials on indictment, there is required a certificate signed by the clerk of the court recording the acquittal or conviction as the case may be, together with the substance of the indictment. Summary verdicts are proved by a copy of the conviction or of the dismissal of the information signed by the clerk of the court.

CHAPTER 39.—ADMISSION OF EXTRINSIC EVIDENCE IN AID OF INTERPRETATION

Rules as to Extrinsic Evidence

Rule I

Evidence of surrounding circumstances admissible to show identity or extent of subject-matter, or meaning of terms

39–23 Note 7. Add: see *Rabin* v. *Gerson Berger Association Ltd.* [1986] 1 All E.R. 374 (C.A.) where it was held that the opinion of counsel was inadmissible for the purposes of assisting in the construction of a document drafted by him.

CHAPTER 41.—WEIGHT OF EVIDENCE: PRESUMPTIONS: ESTOPPELS

2.—Presumptions

Presumptions of fact

41–22A For conflicting presumptions see text, § 4–30, and *R.* v. *Yacoob* (1981) 72 Cr.App.R. 13 (C.A.).

3. Estoppels

(1) Introductory

41–23 Note 30. Add: M. P. Thompson, "From Representation to Expectation: Estoppel as a Cause of Action" [1983] 42 C.L.J. 257.

Note 32. Add: *Avon C.C.* v. *Howlett* [1983] 1 W.L.R. 605 (C.A.), where it was said that estoppel is a rule of evidence.

41–24 Note 34. Add: the *Pacol* case (see text) has now been reported: see *The Henrik Sif* [1982] 1 Lloyd's Rep. 456.

(2) Legal estoppels

41–27 Note 46. Add: In *Keen* v. *Holland* [1984] 1 W.L.R. 251 (C.A.) a landlord and a tenant agreed on a form of extension of the tenancy which enabled the tenant to hold over after the time when the landlord could have evicted him. So as to ensure that the landlord was not prejudiced by thus abandoning his rights, the parties entered into an agreement which was thought to circumvent the protective legislation relating to agricultural tenancies. When later the landlord sought to recover possession, the tenant invoked the legislation, and was held to be protected by it. It was held that it could not be unconscionable for the tenant to rely on the statute, because the latter was designed for protection of tenants, and that there could be no estoppel by convention which prevented the statute from operating where there could have been no express agreement which would have achieved the result desired by the parties. While the decision appears, with respect, to be sound in its analysis of the effect of the statute, it raises difficult questions with regard to estoppel by convention generally. The first of the above propositions demonstrates how far equitable estoppel has been commixed with conventional estoppel by conduct. But it is rather curious equity which recognises only the general intention of a statute in relation to a particular class of persons, in this case agricultural tenants, and ignores the particular circumstances and knowledge of the individual tenant against whom the equity is invoked. Moreover, the court was at pains to point out that the mere fact that *one* of the parties (the landlords) would not have entered into the arrangement if they had not believed that it achieved the desired result could not give rise to an estoppel. This is surely besides the point. The estoppel would not have arisen from the landlords' belief in any event: it would have been based on the fact that the tenant so conducted himself as to induce the belief and knew both of the belief and of the landlords' reliance on it. This would be so even if the tenant himself did not share the belief. See Spencer Bower and Turner, § 160.

4. *A deed which can take effect by interest is not to be construed to take effect by estoppel*

41–33 NOTE 89. See above § 41–24, note 34.

(c) *Estoppels by conduct*

(i) *From agreement*

41–37 NOTE 3. Add: parties deal with each other on the footing of a shared though erroneous assumption, one may be estopped from later proceeding on the basis of the true facts; and this is so even though the party relying on the assumption did not come to hold it by reason of any representation by the other party: *the Leila* [1985] 2 Lloyd's Rep. 172.

Election

41–40 NOTE 30. Thus where a Plaintiff was refused an order of specific performance, but was awarded damages, his appeal against the refusal of specific performance was (in effect) dismissed because he had begun enforcement proceedings against the Defendant before his appeal was heard: *Meng Leong Ltd.* v. *Jip Hong Ltd.* [1984] 3 W.L.R. 1263.

(ii) *Misrepresentation or negligence*

41–41 NOTE 50. Add: If A is entitled to payment from B, and the latter makes an overpayment as a result of which A is induced to believe that the payment is his entitlement, and acts upon that assumption to his detriment, B will be estopped from recovering the overpayment, because the overpayment amounts to a representation of fact: *Avon C.C.* v. *Howlett* [1983] 1 W.L.R. 605 (C.A.) (*cf. Kelly* v. *Solari* (1841) 9 M. & W. 54). It was also held that estoppels are indivisible, so that if a payee acts to his detriment as a result of a payment of money, the whole sum is irrecoverable. It may be that in certain circumstances it would be so unconscionable for the payee to retain the whole of the sum paid to him that he cannot rely on the estoppel at all. The all-or-nothing principle would thus be maintained, but the estoppel would be of no effect.

The fact that a party who is contractually obliged to indemnify a person against certain liabilities refuses to take over the conduct of the defence of proceedings against that person does not result in any estoppel against him. He is entitled thereafter to challenge the validity of any judgment or settlement when a claim is made against him for indemnification: *the C. Joyce* [1986] 2 All E.R. 177.

(3) *Equitable estoppel*

41–42 NOTE 53. Add: *The Scaptrade* [1983] Q.B. 529 (C.A.) (the point was not considered in the House of Lords). The formulation of the principle by Lord Denning M.R. in the *Texas Bank* case [1982] Q.B. 84 at 121–2 was criticised as too broad in *Keen* v. *Holland* (*supra* § 42–27). In *the Leila* [1985] 2 Lloyd's Rep. 172

an estoppel by convention was held to exist (*supra* § 41–37) where there was no equitable estoppel.

NOTE 54. Add: see also *Greasley* v. *Cooke* (text, n. 46); and *cf. Watkins* v. *Elmslie* [1982] 261 E.G. 1192 (C.A.) in which that decision was distinguished and no estoppel found. The principle of proprietary estoppel is capable of extending to the *disposal* of an interest in land, where that disposal is linked to an acquisition of a title to land by a single overall arrangement.

See *Licences and Land Law: Legal Principles and Public Policy* (1984) 100 L.Q.R. 376 (Stephen Moriarty) where it is argued that the difference (or one difference) between promissory and proprietary estoppel is that the former is available only as a shield, whereas the latter is capable of founding a cause of action. See *Maharaj* v. *Chard* [1986] 3 W.L.R. 440 (P.C.), a man was held to have created by promissory estoppel a personal right in the woman with whom he was living and by whom he had a number of children by his representations to her and her reliance on them. It is noteworthy (a) that the estoppel was held not to infringe a statutory prohibition on the creation of interests in land because it was purely a personal right to which it gave rise; and (b) that there is no suggestion in the opinion of the Privy Council that the estoppel was suspensory only, and it seems that it could not be determined by reasonable notice, though presumably it would not survive the death of the mistress.

NOTE 55. Add: *The Henrik Sif* (*supra* § 41–24). *The August Leonhardt* [1984] 1 Lloyd's Rep. 322 followed the *Henrik Sif* (*supra*) but was reversed in the Court of Appeal ([1985] 2 Lloyd's Rep. 28) without the earlier case being mentioned in the appellate judgments. Our doubts as to the correctness of the decision in *The Henrik Sif* were stilled by the fact that another commercial judge had reached the same result. The authority of that case must now again be in doubt. The limits of the doctrine of equitable estoppel were considered in *Drexel* v. *El Nasr* [1986] 1 Lloyd's Rep. 356 at 365–6. See also *B.P. Exploration Co. (Libya) Ltd.* v. *Hunt (No. 2)* [1979] 1 W.L.R. 783 at 810 and the *Texas Bank* case [1982] Q.B. 84 at 103.

APPENDIX

POLICE AND CRIMINAL EVIDENCE ACT 1984

PART V

QUESTIONING AND TREATMENT OF PERSONS BY POLICE

Abolition of certain powers of constables to search persons

42–63 53.—(1) Subject to subsection (2) below, there shall cease to have effect any Act (including a local Act) passed before this Act is so far as it authorises—

(*a*) any search by a constable of a person in police detention at a police station; or

(*b*) an intimate search of a person by a constable,

and any rule of common law which authorises a search such as is mentioned in paragraph (*a*) of (*b*) above is abolished.

(2) Nothing in subsection (1)(*a*) above shall affect paragraph 6(2) of Schedule 3 to the Prevention of Terrorism (Temporary Provisions) Act 1984.

Searches of detained persons

42–64 54.—(1) The custody officer at a police station shall ascertain and record or cause to be recorded everything which a person has with him when he is—

(*a*) brought to the station after being arrested elsewhere or after being committed to custody by an order or sentence of a court; or

(*b*) arrested at the station after

(i) having attended voluntarily there or

(ii) having accompanied a constable there without having been arrested.

(2) In the case of an arrested person the record shall be made as part of his custody record.

(3) Subject to subsection (4) below, a custody officer may seize and retain any such thing or cause any such thing to be seized and retained.

(4) Clothes and personal effects may only be seized if the custody officer—

(*a*) believes that the person from whom they are seized may use them—

(i) to cause physical injury to himself or any other person;

(ii) to damage property;

(iii) to interfere with evidence; or

(iv) to assist him to escape; or

(*b*) has reasonable grounds for believing that they may be evidence relating to an offence.

(5) Where anything is seized, the person from whom it is seized shall be told the reason for the seizure unless he is—

(*a*) violent or likely to become violent; or

(*b*) incapable of understanding what is said to him.

(6) Subject to subsection (7) below, a person may be searched if the custody officer considers it necessary to enable him to carry out his duty under subsection (1) above and to the extent that the custody officer considers necessary for that purpose.

(7) An imtimate search may not be conducted under this section.

(8) A search under this section shall be carried out by a constable.

(9) The constable carrying out a search shall be of the same sex as the person searched.

Intimate searches

42–65 55.—(1) Subject to the following provisions of this section if an officer of at least the rank of superintendent has reasonable grounds for believing—

(*a*) that a person who has been arrested and is in police detention may have concealed on him anything which

(i) he could use to cause physical injury to himself or others; and

(ii) he might so use while he is detention or in the custody of a court; or

(*b*) that such a person—

(i) may have a Class A drug concealed on him; and

(ii) was in possession of it with the appropriate criminal intent before his arrest,

he may authorise such a search of that person.

(2) An officer may not authorise an intimate search of a person for anything unless he has reasonable grounds for believing that it cannot be found without his being intimately searched.

(3) An officer may give an authorisation under subsection (1) above orally or

in writing but, if he gives it orally, he shall confirm it in writing as soon as is practicable.

(4) An intimate search which is only a drug offence shall be way of examination by a suitably qualified person.

(5) Except as provided by subsection (4) above, an intimate search shall be by way of examination by a suitably qualified person unless an officer of a least the rank of superintendent considers that this is not practicable.

(6) An intimate search which is not carried out as mentioned in subsection (5) above shall be carried out by constable.

(7) A constable may not carry out an intimate search of a person of the opposite sex.

(8) No intimate search may be carried out except—

(*a*) at police station;

(*b*) at a hospital;

(*c*) at a registered medical practitioner's surgery; or

(*d*) at some other place used for medical purposes.

(9) An intimate search which is only a drug offence search may not be carried out at a police station.

(10) If an intimate seach of a person is carried out, the custody record relating to him shall state—

(*a*) which parts of his body were searched; and

(*b*) why they were searched.

(11) The information required to be recorded by subsection (10) above shall be recorded as soon as practicable after the completion of the search.

(12) The custody officer at a police station may seize and retain anything which is found on an intimate search of a person, or cause any such thing to be seized and retained—

(*a*) if he believes that the person from whom it is seized may use it—

(i) to cause physical injury to himself or any other person;

(ii) to damage property;

(iii) to interfere with evidence; or

(iv) to assist him to escape; or

(*b*) if he has reasonable grounds for believing that it may be evidence relating to an offence.

(13) Where anything is seized under this section, the person from whom it is seized shall be told the reason for the seizure unless he is

(*a*) violent or likely to become violent; or

(*b*) incapable of understanding what is said to him.

(14) Every annual report—

(*a* under section 12 of the Police Act 1964; or

(*b*) made by the Commissioner of the Metropolis,

shall contain information about searches under this section which have been carried out in the area to which the report relates during the period to which it relates.

(15) The information about such searches shall include—

(*a*) the total number of searches;

(*b*) the number of searches conducted by way of examination by a suitably qualified person;

(*c*) the number of searches not so conducted but conducted in the presence of such a person; and

(*d*) the result of the searches carried out.

(16) The information shall also include, as separate items—

(*a*) the total number of drug offence searches; and
(*b*) the result of those searches.

(17) In this section—

"the appropriate criminal intent" means an intent to commit an offence under—

(*a*) section 5(3) of the Misuse of Drugs Act 1971 (possession of controlled drug with intent to supply to another); or

(*b*) section 68(2) of the Customs and Excise Management Act 1979 (exportation etc. with intent to evade a prohibition or restriction);

"Class A drug" has the meaning assigned to it by section 2(1)(*b*) of the Misuse of Drugs Act 1971;

"drug offence search" means an intimate search for a Class A drug which an officer has authorised by virtue of subsection (1)(*b*) above; and

"suitably qualified person" means—

(*a*) a registered medical practitioner; or
(*b*) a registered nurse.

Fingerprinting

42–66 61.—(1) Except as provided by this section no person's fingerprints may be taken without the appropriate consent.

(2) Consent to the taking of a person's fingerprints must be in writing if it is given at a time when he is at a police station.

(3) The fingerprints of a person detained at a police station may be taken without the appropriate consent—

(*a*) if an officer of at least the rank of superintendent authorises them to be taken; or

(*b*) if—

(i) he has been charged with a recordable offence or informed that he will be reported for such an offence; and

(ii) he has not had his fingerprints taken in the course of the investigation of the offence by the police.

(4) An officer may only give an authorisation under subsection (3)(*a*) above if he has reasonable grounds—

(*a*) for suspecting the involvement of the person whose fingerprints are to be taken in a criminal offence; and

(*b*) for believing that his fingerprints will tend to confirm or disprove his involvement.

(5) An officer may give an authorisation under subsection (3)(*a*) above orally or in writing but, if he gives it orally, he shall confirm it in writing as soon as is practicable.

(6) Any person's fingerprints may be taken without the appropriate consent if he has been convicted of a recordable offence.

(7) In a case where by virtue of subsection (3) or (6) above a person's fingerprints are taken without the appropriate consent—

(*a*) he shall be told the reason before his fingerprints are taken; and

(*b*) the reason shall be recorded as soon as is practicable after the fingerprints are taken.

(8) If he is detained at a police station when the fingerprints are taken, the reason for taking them shall be recorded on his custody record.

(9) Nothing in this section—

(*a*) affects any power conferred by paragraph 18(2) of Schedule 2 to the Immigration Act 1971; or

(*b*) applies to a person arrested or detained under the terrorism provisions.

Fingerprints and samples—supplementary

42–67 65. In this part of this Act—

"appropriate consent" means—

(*a*) in relation to a person who has attained the age of 17 years, the consent of that person;

(*b*) in relation to a person who has not attained that age but has attained the age of 14 years, the consent of that person and his parent or guardian; and

(*c*) in relation to a person who has not attained the age of 14 years, the consent of his parent or guardian;

"fingerprints" includes palm prints;

"intimate sample" means a sample of blood, semen or any other tissue fluid, urine, saliva or pubic hair, or a swab taken from a person's body orifice

"non-intimate sample" means—

(*a*) a sample of hair other than pubic hair,

(*b*) a sample taken from a nail or from under a nail;

(*c*) a swab taken from any part of a person's body other than a body orifice;

(*d*) a footprint or a similar impression of any part of a person's body other than a part of his hand;

"the terrorism provisions" means—

(*a*) section 12(1) of the Prevention of Terrorism (Temporary Provisions) Act 1984; and

(*b*) any provision conferring a power of arrest or detention and contained in an order under section 13 of that Act; and

"terrorism" has the meaning assigned to it by section 14(1) of that Act.

PART VII

DOCUMENTARY EVIDENCE IN CRIMINAL PROCEEDINGS

Evidence from documentary records

42–68 68.—(1) Subject to section 69 below, a statement in a document shall be admissible in any proceedings as evidence of any fact stated therein of which direct oral evidence would be admissible if—

(*a*) the document is or forms part of a record compiled by a person acting under a duty from information supplied by a person (whether acting under a duty or not) who had, or may reasonably be supposed to have had, personal knowledge of the matters dealt with in that information; and

(*b*) any condition relating to the person who supplied the information which is specified in subsection (2) below is satisfied.

(2) The conditions mentioned in subsection (1)(*b*) above are—

(*a*) that the person who supplied the information—

(i) is dead or by reason of his bodily or mental condition unfit to attend as a witness;

(ii) is outside the United Kingdom and it is not reasonably practicable to secure his attendance; or

(iii) cannot reasonably be expected (having regard to the time which has elapsed since he supplied or acquired the information and to all the circumstances) to have any recollection of the matters dealt with in that information;

(*b*) that all reasonable steps have been taken to identify the person who supplied the information but that he cannot be identified; and

(*c*) that, the identity of the person who supplied the information being known, all reasonable steps have been taken to find him, but that he cannot be found.

(3) Nothing in this section shall prejudice the admissibility of any evidence that would be admissible apart from this section.

Evidence from computer records

42–69 69.—(1) In any proceedings, a statement in a document produced by a computer shall not be admissible as evidence of any fact stated therein unless it is shown—

(*a*) that there are no reasonable grounds for believing that the statement is inaccurate because of improper use of the computer;

(*b*) that at all material times the computer was operating properly, or if not, that any respect in which it was not operating properly or was out of operation was not such as to affect the production of the document or the accuracy of its contents; and

(*c*) that any relevant conditions specified in rules of court under subsection (2) below are satisfied.

(2) Provision may be made by rules of court requiring that in any proceedings where it is desired to give a statement in evidence by virtue of this section such information concerning the statement as may be required by the rules shall be provided in such form and at such time as may be so required.

Provisions supplementary to Sections 68 and 69

42–70 70.—(1) Part I of Schedule 3 to this Act shall have effect for the purpose of supplementing section 68 above.

(2) Part II of that Schedule shall have effect for the purpose of supplementing section 69 above.

(3) Part III of that Schedule shall have effect for the purpose of supplementing both sections.

Microfilm copies

42–71 71. In any proceedings the contents of a document may (whether or not the document is still in existence) be proved by the production of an enlargement of a microfilm copy of that document or of the material part of it, authenticated in such manner as the court may approve.

Part VII—Supplementary

42–72 72.—(1) In this Part of this Act—

"copy" and "statement" have the same meanings as in Part I of the Civil Evidence Act 1968; and

"proceedings" means criminal proceedings, including—

(*a*) proceedings in the United Kingdom or elsewhere before a court-martial constituted under the Army Act 1955 or the Air Force Act 1955;

(*b*) proceedings in the United Kingdom or elsewhere before the Courts-Martial Appeal Court—

(i) on an appeal from a court-martial so constituted or from a court-martial constituted under the Naval Discipline Act 1957; or

(ii) on a reference under section 34 of the Courts-Martial (Appeals) Act 1968; and

(*c*) proceedings before a Standing Civilian Court.

(2) Nothing in this Part of this Act shall prejudice any power of a court to exclude evidence (whether by preventing questions from being put or otherwise) at its discretion.

PART VIII

EVIDENCE IN CRIMINAL PROCEEDINGS—GENERAL

Convictions and acquittals

Proof of convictions and acquittals

42–73 73.—(1) Where in any proceedings the fact that a person has in the United Kingdom been convicted or acquitted of an offence otherwise than by a Service court is admissible in evidence, it may be proved by producing a certificate of conviction or, as the case may be, of acquittal relating to that offence, and proving that the person named in the certificate as having been convicted or acquitted of the offence is the person whose conviction or acquittal of the offence is to be proved.

(2) For the purposes of this section a certificate of conviction or of acquittal—

(*a*) shall, as regards a conviction or acquittal on indictment, consist of a certificate, signed by the clerk of the court where the conviction or acquittal took place, giving the substance and effect (omitting the formal parts) of the indictment and of the conviction or acquittal; and

(*b*) shall, as regards a conviction or acquittal on a summary trial, consist of a copy of the conviction or of the dismissal of the information, signed by the clerk of the court where the conviction or acquittal took place or by the clerk of the court, if any, to which a memorandum of the conviction or acquittal was sent;

and a document purporting to be a duly signed certificate of conviction or acquittal under this section shall be taken to be such a certificate unless the contrary is proved.

(3) References in this section to the clerk of a court include references to his deputy and to any other person having the custody of the court record.

(4) The method of proving a conviction or acquittal authorised by this section shall be in addition to and not to the exclusion of any other authorised manner of proving a conviction or acquittal.

Conviction as evidence of commission of offence

42–74 74.—(1) In any proceedings the fact that a person other than the accused has been convicted of an offence by or before any court in the United Kingdom or by a Service court outside the United Kingdom shall be admissible in evidence for the purpose of proving, where to do so is relevant to any issue in those proceedings, that that person committed that offence, whether or not any other evidence of his having committed that offence is given.

(2) In any proceedings in which by virtue of this section a person other than the accused is proved to have been convicted of an offence by or before any court in the United Kingdom or by a Service court outside the United Kingdom, he shall be taken to have committed that offence unless the contrary is proved.

(3) In any proceedings where evidence is admissible of the fact that the accused has committed an offence, in so far as that evidence is relevant to any matter in issue in the proceedings for a reason other than a tendency to show in the accused a disposition to commit the kind of offence with which he is charged, if the accused is proved to have been convicted of the offence—

(*a*) by or before any court in the United Kingdom; or

(*b*) by a Service court outside the United Kingdom,

he shall be taken to have committed that offence unless the contrary is proved.

(4) Nothing in this section shall prejudice—

(*a*) the admissibility in evidence of any conviction which would be admissible apart from this section; or

(*b*) the operation of any enactment whereby a conviction or a finding of fact in any proceedings is for the purposes of any other proceedings made conclusive evidence of any fact.

Provisions supplementary to section 74

42–75 75.—(1) Where evidence that a person has been convicted of an offence is admissible by virtue of section 74 above, then without prejudice to the reception of any other admissible evidence for the purpose of identifying the facts on which the conviction was based—

(*a*) the contents of any document which is admissible as evidence of the conviction; and

(*b*) the contents of the information, complaint, indictment or charge-sheet on which the person in question was convicted,

shall be admissible in evidence for that purpose.

(2) Where in any proceedings the contents of any document are admissible in evidence by virtue of subsection (1) above, a copy of that document, or of the material part of it, purporting to be certified or otherwise authenticated by or on behalf of the court or authority having custody of that document shall be admissible in evidence and shall be taken to be a true copy of that document or part unless the contrary is shown.

(3) Nothing in any of the following—

(*a*) section 13 of the Powers of Criminal Courts Act 1973 (under which a conviction leading to probation or discharge is to be disregarded except as mentioned in that section);

(*b*) section 392 of the Criminal Procedure (Scotland) Act 1975 (which makes similar provision in respect of convictions on indictment in Scotland); and

(*c*) section 8 of the Probation Act (Northern Ireland) 1950 (which corresponds to section 13 of the Powers of Criminal Courts Act 1973) or any legislation which is in force in Northern Ireland for the time being and corresponds to that section,

shall affect the operation of section 74 above; and for the purposes of that section any order made by a court of summary jurisdiction in Scotland under section 182 or section 183 of the said Act of 1975 shall be treated as a conviction.

(4) Nothing in section 74 above shall be construed as rendering admissible in any proceedings evidence of any conviction other than a subsisting one.

Confessions

42–76 76.—(1) In any proceedings a confession made by an accused person may be given in evidence against him in so far as it is relevant to any matter in issue in the proceedings and is not excluded by the court in pursuance of this section.

(2) If, in any proceedings where the prosecution proposes to give in evidence a confession made by an accused person, it is represented to the court that the confession was or may have been obtained—

(*a*) by oppression of the person who made it; or

(*b*) in consequence of anything said or done which was likely, in the circumstances existing at the time, to render unreliable any confession which might be made by him in consequence thereof,

the court shall not allow the confession to be given in evidence against him except in so far as the prosecution proves to the court beyond reasonable doubt that the confession (notwithstanding that it may be true) was not obtained as aforesaid.

(3) In any proceedings where the prosecution proposes to give in evidence a confession made by an accused person, the court may of its own motion require the prosecution, as a condition of allowing it to do so, to prove that the confession was not obtained as mentioned in subsection (2) above.

(4) The fact that a confession is wholly or partly excluded in pursuance of this section shall not affect the admissibility in evidence—

(*a*) of any facts discovered as a result of the confession; or

(*b*) where the confession is relevant as showing that the accused speaks, writes or expresses himself in a particular way, of so much of the confession as is necessary to show that he does so.

(5) Evidence that a fact to which this subsection applies was discovered as a result of a statement made by an accused person shall not be admissible unless evidence of how it was discovered is given by him or on his behalf.

(6) Subsection (5) above applies—

(*a*) to any fact discovered as a result of a confession which is wholly excluded in pursuance of this section; and

(*b*) to any fact discovered as a result of a confession which is partly so excluded, if the fact is discovered as a result of the excluded part of the confession.

(7) Nothing in Part VII of this Act shall prejudice the admissibility of a confession made by an accused person.

(8) In this section "oppression" includes torture, inhuman or degrading treatment, and the use or threat of violence (whether or not amounting to torture).

Confessions by mentally handicapped persons

42–77 77.—(1) Without prejudice to the general duty of the court at a trial on indictment to direct the jury on any matter on which it appears to the court appropriate to do so, where at such a trial—

(*a*) the case against the accused depends wholly or substantially on a confession by him; and

(*b*) the court is satisfied—

(i) that he is mentally handicapped; and

(ii) that the confession was not made in the presence of an independent person,

the court shall warn the jury that there is special need for caution before convicting the accused in reliance on the confession, and shall explain that the need arises because of the circumstances mentioned in paragraphs (*a*) and (*b*) above.

(2) In any case where at the summary trial of a person for an offence it appears to the court that a warning under subsection (1) above would be required if the trial were on indictment, the court shall treat the case as one in which there is a special need for caution before convicting the accused on his confession.

(3) In this section—

"independent person" does not include a police officer or a person employed for, or engaged on, police purposes;

"mentally handicapped," in relation to a person, means that he is in a state of arrested or incomplete development of mind which includes significant impairment of intelligence and social functioning; and

"police purposes" has the meaning assigned to it by section 64 of the Police Act 1964.

Miscellaneous

Exclusion of unfair evidence

42–78 78.—(1) In any proceedings the court may refuse to allow evidence on which the prosecution proposes to rely to be given if it appears to the court that, having regard to all the circumstances, including the circumstances in which the evidence was obtained, the admission of the evidence would have such an adverse effect on the fairness of the proceedings that the court ought not to admit it.

(2) Nothing in this section shall prejudice any rule of law requiring a court to exclude evidence.

Time for taking accused's evidence

42–79 79. If at the trial of any person for an offence—

(*a*) the defence intends to call two or more witnesses to the facts of the case; and

(*b*) those witnesses include the accused,

the accused shall be called before the other witness or witnesses unless the court in its discretion otherwise directs.

Competence and compellability of accused's spouse

42–80 80.—(1) In any proceedings the wife or husband of the accused shall be competent to give evidence—

(*a*) subject to subsection (4) below, for the prosecution; and

(*b*) on behalf of the accused or any person jointly charged with the accused.

(2) In any proceedings the wife or husband of the accused shall, subject to subsection (4) below, be compellable to give evidence on behalf of the accused.

(3) In any proceedings the wife or husband of the accused shall, subject to subsection (4) below, be compellable to give evidence for the prosecution or on behalf of any person jointly charged with the accused if and only if—

(*a*) the offence charged involved an assault on, or injury or a threat of injury to, the wife or husband of the accused or a person who was at the material time under the age of sixteen; or

(*b*) the offence charged is a sexual offence alleged to have been committed in respect of a person who was at the material time under that age; or

(*c*) the offence charged consists of attempting or conspiring to commit, or of aiding, abetting, counselling, procuring or inciting the commission of, an offence falling within paragraph (*a*) or (*b*) above.

(4) Where a husband and wife are jointly charged with an offence neither spouse shall at the trial be competent or compellable by virtue of subsection (1)(*a*), (2) or (3) above to give evidence in respect of that offence unless that spouse is not, or is no longer, liable to be convicted of that offence at the trial as a result of pleading guilty or for any other reason.

(5) In any proceedings a person who has been but is no longer married to the accused shall be competent and compellable to give evidence as if that person and the accused had never been married.

(6) Where in any proceedings the age of any person at any time is material for the purposes of subsection (3) above, his age at the material time shall for the purposes of that provision be deemed to be or to have been that which appears to the court to be or to have been his age at that time.

(7) In subsection (3)(*b*) above "sexual offence" means an offence under the Sexual Offences Act 1956, the Indecency with Children Act 1960, the Sexual Offences Act 1967, section 54 of the Criminal Law Act 1977 or the Protection of Children Act 1978.

(8) The failure of the wife or husband of the accused to give evidence shall not be made the subject of any comment by the prosecution.

(9) Section 1(*d*) of the Criminal Evidence Act 1898 (communications between husband and wife) and section 43(1) of the Matrimonial Causes Act 1965 (evidence as to marital intercourse) shall cease to have effect.

Advance notice of expert evidence in Crown Court

42–81 81.—(1) Crown Court Rules may make provision for—

(*a*) requiring any party to proceedings before the court to disclose to the other party or parties any expert evidence which he proposes to adduce in the proceedings; and

(*b*) prohibiting a party who fails to comply in respect of any evidence with any requirement imposed by virtue of paragraph (*a*) above from adducing that evidence without the leave of the court.

(2) Crown Court Rules made by virtue of this section may specify the kinds of expert evidence to which they apply and may exempt facts or matters of any description specified in the rules.

Part VIII—supplementary

Interpretation

42–82 82.—(1) In this Part of this Act—

"confession," includes any statement wholly or partly adverse to the person who made it, whether made to a person in authority or not and whether made in words or otherwise;

"court-martial" means a court-martial constituted under the Army Act 1955, the Air Force Act 1955 or the Naval Discipline Act 1957 or a disciplinary court constituted under section 50 of the said Act of 1957;

"proceedings" means criminal proceedings, including—

(*a*) proceedings in the United Kingdom or elsewhere before a court-martial constituted under the Army Act 1955 or the Air Force Act 1955;

(*b*) proceedings in the United Kingdom or elsewhere before the Courts-Martial Appeal Court—

(i) on an appeal from a court-martial so constituted or from a court-martial constituted under the Naval Discipline Act 1957; or

(ii) on a reference under section 34 of the Courts-Martial (Appeals) Act 1968; and

(*c*) proceedings before a Standing Civilian Court; and

"Service court" means a court-martial or a Standing Civilian Court.

(2) In this Part of this Act references to conviction before a Service court are references—

(*a*) as regards a court-martial constituted under the Army Act 1955 or the Air Force Act 1955, to a finding of guilty which is, or falls to be treated as, a finding of the court duly confirmed;

(*b*) as regards—

(i) a court-martial; or

(ii) a disciplinary court,

constituted under the Naval Discipline Act 1957, to a finding of guilty which is, or falls to be treated as, the finding of the court;

and "convicted" shall be construed accordingly.

(3) Nothing in this Part of this Act shall prejudice any power of a court to exclude evidence (whether by preventing questions from being put or otherwise) at its discretion.

SCHEDULE 3

Provisions Supplementary to Sections 68 and 69

Part I

Provisions Supplementary to Section 68

42–83 1. Section 68(1) above applies whether the information contained in the document was supplied directly or indirectly but, if it was supplied indirectly, only if each person through whom it was supplied was acting under a duty; and applies also where the person compiling the record is himself the person by whom the information is supplied.

2. Where—

(*a*) a document setting out the evidence which a person could be expected to give as a witness has been prepared for the purpose of any pending or contemplated proceedings; and

(*b*) it falls within subsection (1) of section 68 above,

a statement contained in it shall not be given in evidence by virtue of that section without the leave of the court, and the court shall not give leave unless it is of the opinion that the statement ought to be admitted in the interests of justice, having regard—

(i) to the circumstances in which leave is sought and in particular to the contents of the statement; and

(ii) to any likelihood that the accused will be prejudiced by its admission in the absence of the person who supplied the information on which it is based.

3. Where in any proceedings a statement based on information supplied by any person is given in evidence by virtue of section 68 above—

(*a*) any evidence which, if that person had been called as a witness, would have been admissible as relevant to his credibility as a witness shall be admissible for that purpose in those proceedings;

(*b*) evidence may, with the leave of the court, be given of any matter which, if that person had been called as a witness, could have been put to him in cross-examination as relevant to his credibility as a witness but of which evidence could not have been adduced by the cross-examining party; and

(*c*) evidence tending to prove that that person, whether before or after supplying the information, made a statement (whether oral or not) which is inconsistent with it shall be admissible for the purpose of showing that he has contradicted himself.

4. A statement which is admissible by virtue of section 68 above shall not be capable of corroborating evidence given by the person who supplied the information on which the statement is based.

5. In deciding for the purposes of section 68(2)(*a*)(i) above whether a person is unfit to attend as a witness the court may act on a certificate purporting to be signed by a registered medical practitioner.

6. Any reference in section 68 above or this Part of this Schedule to a person acting under a duty includes a reference to a person acting in the course of any trade, business, profession or other occupation in which he is engaged or employed or for the purposes of any paid or unpaid office held by him.

7. In estimating the weight, if any, to be attached to a statement admissible in evidence by virtue of section 68 above regard shall be had to all the circumstances from which any inference can reasonably be drawn as to the accuracy or otherwise of the statement and, in particular—

(*a*) to the question whether or not the person who supplied the information from which the record containing the statement was compiled did so contemporaneously with the occurrence or existence of the facts dealt with in that information; and

(*b*) to the question whether or not that person, or any other person concerned with compiling or keeping the record containing the statement, had any incentive to conceal or misrepresent the facts.

Part II

Provisions Supplementary to Section 69

42–84 8. In any proceedings where it is desired to give a statement in evidence in accordance with section 69 above, a certificate—

(*a*) identifying the document containing the statement and describing the manner in which it was produced;

(*b*) giving such particulars of any device involved in the production of that document as may be appropriate for the purpose of showing that the document was produced by a computer;

(*c*) dealing with any of the matters mentioned in subsection (1) of section 69 above; and

(*d*) purporting to be signed by a person occupying a responsible position in relation to the operation of the computer,

shall be evidence of anything stated in it; and for the purposes of this paragraph it shall be sufficient for a matter to be stated to the best of the knowledge and belief of the person stating it.

9. Notwithstanding paragraph 8 above, a court may require oral evidence to

be given of anything of which evidence could be given by a certificate under that paragraph.

10. Any person who in a certificate tendered under paragraph 8 above in a magistrates' court, the Crown Court or the Court of Appeal makes a statement which he knows to be false or does not believe to be true shall be guilty of an offence and liable—

(*a*) on conviction on indictment to imprisonment for a term not exceeding two years or to a fine or to both;

(*b*) on summary conviction to imprisonment for a term not exceeding six months or to a fine not exceeding the statutory maximum (as defined in section 74 of the Criminal Justice Act 1982) or to both.

11. In estimating the weight, if any, to be attached to a statement regard shall be had to all the circumstances from which any inference can reasonably be drawn as to the accuracy or otherwise of the statement and, in particular—

(*a*) to the question whether or not the information which the information contained in the statement reproduces or is derived from was supplied to the relevant computer, or recorded for the purpose of being supplied to it, contemporaneously with the occurrence or existence of the facts dealt with in that information; and

(*b*) to the question whether or not any person concerned with the supply of information to that computer, or with the operation of that computer or any equipment by means of which the document containing the statement was produced by it, had any incentive to conceal or misrepresent the facts.

12. For the purposes of paragraph 11 above information shall be taken to be supplied to a computer whether it is supplied directly or (with or without human intervention) by means of any appropriate equipment.

PART III

PROVISIONS SUPPLEMENTARY TO SECTIONS 68 AND 69

42–85 13. Where in any proceedings a statement contained in a document is admissible in evidence by virtue of section 68 above or in accordance with section 69 above it may be proved—

(*a*) by the production of that document; or

(*b*) (whether or not that document is still in existence) by the production of a copy of that document, or of the material part of it,

authenticated in such manner as the court may approve.

14. For the purpose of deciding whether or not a statement is so admissible the court may draw any reasonable inference—

(*a*) from the circumstances in which the statement was made or otherwise came into being; or

(*b*) from any other circumstances, including the form and contents of the document in which the statement is contained.

15. Provision may be made by rules of court for supplementing the provisions of section 68 or 69 above or this Schedule.